HOW TO DRAW
CARTOONS

Judy Tatchell

Designed by Graham Ro
Illustrated by Graham Round, T
Robert Walster and Chris

Additional designs by Brian Robertson and Camilla Luff

CONTENTS

2 About cartoons
3 First faces
4 Cartoon people
6 Making faces
7 More expressions
8 Drawing from different sides
10 Moving pictures
11 More movement

12 Drawing stereotypes
13 Scenery and perspective
14 Cartoon jokes
16 Short comic strips
18 Long comic strips
20 Special effects
22 Drawing animals
23 Internet links

About cartoons

Caricature

Cartoons look quick and easy to draw. You may have found that they are not as easy as they look, though. The first part of this book is full of simple ways to draw good cartoons.

Pages 3-13 tell you how to draw cartoon people using simple shapes and lines. You can find out how to draw expressions and show movement, too.

You can also use cartoon techniques to draw caricatures. A caricature is a funny picture of a real person. To draw them, you exaggerate things, such as the shape of their nose or hair.

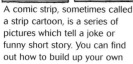

A comic book

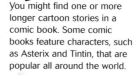

A comic strip, sometimes called a strip cartoon, is a series of pictures which tell a joke or funny short story. You can find out how to build up your own comic strips on pages 16-19.

You might find one or more longer cartoon stories in a comic book. Some comic books feature characters, such as Asterix and Tintin, that are popular all around the world.

Cartoons can also be made into films for movies or television. Cartoon films are called animation, which means "the giving of life". Cartoons are brought to life in a film.

You can use any of the pictures marked with this symbol as clip art on your computer. To download them, go to www.usborne-quicklinks.com

THE USBORNE
Pocket Artist

CONTENTS

Part One:	How to draw cartoons	1
Part Two:	How to draw dinosaurs	25
Part Three:	How to draw monsters	49
Part Four:	How to draw machines	73
Part Five:	How to draw ghosts	97
Part Six:	How to draw animals	121
Part Seven:	How to draw people	145
Part Eight:	How to draw cats	169
Part Nine:	How to draw horses	193
Part Ten:	How to draw maps	217
Part Eleven:	How to draw buildings	241
Part Twelve:	How to draw spacecraft	265

First faces

This page shows you an easy way to draw cartoon faces. All you need is a pencil and a sheet of paper. If you want to color the faces in, you can use colored pencils or felt-tip pens.

Faces to copy

Here are some more faces for you to copy. You can see how in a cartoon some things are exaggerated, such as the size of the nose or the expression.

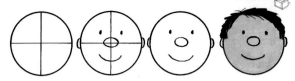

Draw a circle. Do two pencil lines crossing it. Put the nose where the lines cross. The ears are level with the nose.

The eyes go slightly above the nose. Erase the lines crossing the face. Add any sort of hair you like, then color the face.

Looking around

 Draw these lines in pencil, so you can erase them later.

 Nose goes where lines cross

Ear moves around

 As the face turns more, this line moves further around

Profile

 This is a side view, or profile. Draw a line across the middle of the head to show you where the nose and ears go.

The first picture shows a face from the front, with lines crossing it. As the face looks to the side, the line going across the face stays where it is. The line going down curves to one side. The curve of the line makes the head look ball-shaped.

 Line curves up in the middle

 The more the face tilts upward, the more the line curves.

 Line curves down in the middle

To draw a face looking up, do a line across the face as shown. The nose goes in the centre and the ears at each end of the line.

For a face looking down, the line curves down in the middle. Can you see how the face looking up and to one side is drawn?

---

*Go to **www.usborne-quicklinks.com** for a link to a Web site where you can learn about line and shape, the basic elements of drawing.*

Cartoon people

Now you can try adding some bodies to your cartoon faces. There are two different methods described on these pages.

The first uses stick figures. The second uses rounded shapes. Try them both and see which you find easier.

Stick figures

Use a pencil, so you can erase the lines later.

Body stick

Keep this line short or the figure will end up bottom-heavy.

Erase a bit of the head line here, where the hair falls forward.

Draw this stick figure. The body stick is slightly longer than the head. The legs are slightly longer than the body. The arms are a little shorter than the legs.

Here are the outlines of some clothes for the figure. You can copy a sweatshirt with jeans or with a skirt. You could also try some overalls or a dress.

To dress your stick figure, draw the clothes around it, starting at the neck and working down. You can add long, short, curly or straight hair.

Drawing hands and feet

When someone is facing you, you can see their thumbs and first fingers.

People's feet usually turn out a little.

Cartoon hands and shoes, like cartoon heads, are larger than on a real person. Practice drawing these shapes before you add them to the figures.

Adding color

Use a fine felt-tip pen for the outline.

A cartoon person's head is larger than a real person's.

Give her socks if you like.

Shiny white patch on shoes

When you have finished the outline of the figure, go over it with a felt-tip pen. Once it is dry, you can erase the stick figure and color the cartoon.

The girl needs some lines for her legs before you can add her shoes. When you color the shoes, leave a small white patch on the toes to make them shiny.

Figures using rounded shapes

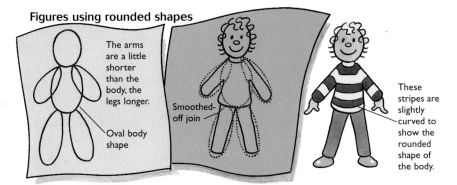

The arms are a little shorter than the body, the legs longer.

Oval body shape

Smoothed-off join

These stripes are slightly curved to show the rounded shape of the body.

With a pencil, draw a head shape. Add an oval for the body and squished ovals for the arms and legs. The body is about one and a half times as long as the head.

Add the outlines of the clothes, smoothing off any joints, such as between the arms or legs and the body. Go over the outline in pen and erase pencil lines.

Add hands and feet and color the figure in. You can find out how to make your cartoon figure look as though it is moving on pages 10-11.

More cartoon people to draw

Try varying your rounded shapes or stick figures to draw all sorts of different-shaped cartoon people.

Tiny person – head larger in proportion to body

Tall person – egg-shaped head and longer body

Fat person – squashed head and shorter legs

Short person – head, body and legs the same length

Some things to try

When you have practiced drawing several figures using the methods shown above, you could try drawing a figure outline right away. If you find it difficult, you can go back to drawing a stick or a rounded shape figure first.

Try drawing all these different people:
• A fat lady wearing a fur coat and hat
• A man with hairy legs wearing shorts
• A boy and a girl in their party clothes.

5

Making faces

You can make cartoon characters come to life by giving them different expressions. These two pages show you how to do this, by adding or changing a few lines.

First, try drawing the faces in pencil. Then you can color them in.

Happy faces

Girls and women tend to have slightly smaller noses than boys and men.

These lines make the ears look more real.

Happiness is shown by drawing a smiling mouth. Drawing the eyes as shown above gives a cheerful expression.

You can make the person burst out laughing by opening the mouth more and showing the teeth.

This is a bigger laugh. The head is thrown back. You can find out how to position the features on page 3.

Sad and angry faces

Sadness and anger are also mainly shown in the eyes and mouth.

Lines show shaking with fury

Sad: the mouth and eyebrows droop.

Angry: use straight lines for the mouth and eyebrows.

Furious: the person frowns and turns red in the face.

Hopping mad: the mouth is wide open in a loud yell.

Go to www.usborne-quicklinks.com for a link to a Web site where you can see lots more ways to draw different expressions.

More expressions

Here are lots more faces for you to practice. You can add bodies in different positions.

Remember that a person's head might be facing you while the body is sideways.

White stripes in hair make it look shiny.

Smug: sideways grin and half-closed eyes.

Winking: mouth tilts up on side while eye is closed.

You can make the face look fatter by adding curves on the cheeks and chin.

Girls' and boys' faces are similar shapes but they can have different hairstyles.

| Suspicious | Scared | Startled | Scheming | Thinking |

Happy   Laughing   Sad   Angry   Crying

Spiky hair   Long hair   Braided hair   Balding head   Woolly hat

Hugging   Thinking   Hands on hips   Waving   Carrying

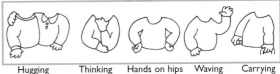

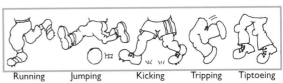

Running   Jumping   Kicking   Tripping   Tiptoeing

Drawing from different sides

Here you can find out how to draw people from the side and from the back as well as from the front. You can also see how to make your pictures more interesting by drawing a bird's-eye view (looking down) or a worm's-eye view (looking up). There are some instructions to help you do this on the opposite page.

Turning around

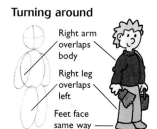

Right arm overlaps body

Right leg overlaps left

Feet face same way

As a person begins to turn around, their body becomes narrower. (See page 3 for how to draw the face.)

Side view

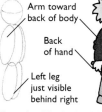

Arm toward back of body

Shape of nose

Back of hand

Left leg just visible behind right

From the side, the body is at its narrowest. You can see the shape of the nose and the back of one hand.

Back view

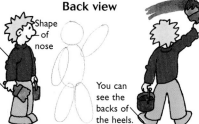

You can see the backs of the heels.

From the back, the body parts are the same sizes and shapes as from the front. The feet turn upward a little.

More positions to draw

Here are lots of cartoon people, in all sorts of positions. Copy them and they will help you draw people in other positions, too.

Sitting on the ground

Piggy-back

On a bicycle

Sitting on a chair

8

A bird's-eye view

A bird's-eye view can make an ordinary picture subject look quite different and dramatic. Try drawing this family group as seen from above.

The parts of the body closer to you are bigger than those further away. Also, the bodies are shorter than if you were drawing them straight on from the front. This is called foreshortening.

Start by drawing a set of pencil lines fanning out from a point. Fit the people roughly in between them.

Heads look biggest as they are closest

Pencil lines help you to get the proportions of the people right.

Bodies get smaller the further away they are

Hints for the pictures

Try to space the lines evenly. This means that all the people will become larger at the same rate.

Big people can slightly overlap the lines, and small people can fall within them.

The longer you draw the people, the more of a worm's-eye view the picture will become. This is also true for a bird's-eye view.

A worm's-eye view

Bodies become smaller the farther away they are, and they are foreshortened.

A worm's-eye view is looking upward from ground level. Draw another set of pencil lines starting from the top. This time, the legs and feet are biggest.

The head of the tallest person is the smallest.

Looking from the bottom, the feet are biggest.

9

Moving pictures

Here, you can find out ways of drawing cartoon people walking, running, jumping and so on. Start with a stick or shape figure if it helps.

Walking and running

The right arm is in front when the left leg is forward.

Use this figure to help you get the body right.

When someone is walking briskly, they lean forward a little. There is always one foot on the ground.

Draw the figure just above ground level to show he is on the move.

Starting to run, the body leans forward even more. The elbows bend and move backward and forward.

Add a few curved lines to show fast movement.

Blobs of sweat flying off head

The faster someone is going, the more the body leans forward and the further the arms stretch.

Jumping

The more this leg bends, the higher the jump will be.

Both feet come forward to hit the ground.

Running toward the jump...   Taking off...   In mid-flight...   Landing from the jump

Falling over

These pictures show a stick person running along and tripping over. Copy them and then fill in the body shapes around the stick figures.

10

More movement

Here are some even more dramatic ways to show movement. You exaggerate certain things to give an impression of lots of speed or effort. You can write words on a picture to give extra impact.

Beads of perspiration

Fists clenched

Legs spinning

You can even add movement lines around the letters.

Clouds of dust

ZOOM!

Make the letters big and bold. You could do them in color.

ZIP!

Wheel spin

The person above is running to catch a bus. You could add words like ZOOM or WHIZZ, with an exclamation mark.

The hair and scarf of the skater on the left are streaming out behind her. This gives a sense of speed.

These figures look like they are running away. The dust clouds get smaller as they get further away.*

The figures are in the distance, so they are small. A curved line for the ground gives a feeling of space.

These silhouettes have long shadows to make it look like evening.

This is called perspective. There is more about it on page 13.

11

Drawing stereotypes

In cartoons, you can show what people do for a living by drawing a kind of caricature called a stereotype. People may be different shapes, have different expressions, move in different ways, wear different clothes and carry different tools, depending on what they do.

You normally recognize a stereotype from the shape of the body and the clothes. Here are a few you might like to try.

Getting started

If you like, draw stick figures or rounded shapes to help you get started on the figure. There is more about this on pages 4-5. Then you can work on the outline and clothes.

Can you see which characters some of these might belong to?

Chef

Chef's hat

Light blue shading on the clothes gives the impression of whiteness.

A stereotyped chef is jolly and round, with a big red face and a mustache.

Burglar

Loot bag

Striped jersey

Flashlight

The burglar creeps along on tiptoe.

No real burglar would wear this kind of outfit, but this is how they are generally drawn in cartoons.

Boxer

Hands in front of face

Opponent knocked out

The boxer is muscular and heavy, with a squished nose and swollen ear. He wears big gloves and laced boots.

Ballerina

These lines show she is pirouetting.

Slender limbs and hands

The ballerina is very slim and light on her feet. She stands on her toes.

12

Scenery and perspective

Scenery and backgrounds can add a lot of information about what is happening in your pictures. You need to keep the scenery quite simple, though, so that characters stand out against it.

Here, you can see how to achieve a sense of distance, or depth, into pictures. This is called drawing in perspective.

Tricks of perspective

The farther away something is, the smaller it looks. The woman in this picture is drawn smaller than the burglar to make her look farther away.

If you draw the woman level with the burglar, it will look like the picture above – she just looks like a tiny person. Draw her higher up to make her look more distant.

Parallel lines appear to get closer the farther away they are. They seem to meet at a point on the horizon. This is called the vanishing point.

A high vanishing point makes it seem as if you are looking down on the picture. What do you think happens if you draw a low vanishing point?

A picture in perspective

Here is a picture in perspective. The woman is drawn smaller and farther up than the burglar to make her look further away.

Vanishing point

Pavement and fence get narrower

Fence posts get closer together

If the vanishing point falls outside your picture area, try sketching it in pencil as above. This helps to get all the lines properly in perspective. You can erase the lines later.

*Go to **www.usborne-quicklinks.com** for a link to a Web site where you can find out more about using perspective in your drawings.*

13

Cartoon jokes

Cartoon jokes are often printed in newspapers and magazines. They may appear as a strip (see pages 16-17) or a single picture, called a single cartoon. The one on the right is a single cartoon.

Here you can find out what kind of jokes make good cartoons, what materials cartoonists use and some tips on drawing single cartoons yourself.

What makes a good single cartoon?

- A lot of information about what is happening and a lot of the humor in the picture itself
- A short caption
- A joke that is quick and easy to understand.

The type of joke that makes a good single cartoon usually has the qualities shown above.

Ideas for jokes

It can be difficult to think up ideas for jokes on the spot. You might find it easier to think first of a theme or a situation. This may then suggest something funny to you.

Here are some common cartoon themes and some jokes based on them.

A desert island

This is one of the most common themes for single cartoon jokes.

A hospital

This joke has two common cartoon themes – hospitals and manhole covers.

Vampires

This is funny because it shows a monstrous creature doing something ordinary.

Materials you can use

The materials shown below are all you need to get started. They are not expensive to buy, and you may already have them anyway. If you like, though, you can buy some of the specialized materials shown on the rest of this page.

Hard   Medium   Soft

Pencils are marked to show how hard or soft they are. Experiment to find a type you like. Pencils range from 12B (very soft) to 12H (very hard).

You can draw on good quality copier paper which is not too expensive.

Felt-tip pens do not smudge or blot. In time, though, you may find that the ink fades in sunlight. If you find it easier, sketch a drawing in pencil first and then go over it with a pen.

How professional cartoonists work

Single cartoons are usually drawn in black and white for printing in newspapers and magazines. Here are some of the materials that cartoonists use.

Drawing pens come with different thicknesses of nibs. They draw a very even line.

Pencils: a cartoonist might use a medium pencil for outlines and a softer one for shading.

Dip pens and Indian ink: you can get different shapes and thicknesses of nib.

Fine paintbrushes

Bristol paper takes pens, pencils or paint equally well.

Mat can have different surfaces, from very smooth and shiny to quite rough and soft.

Felt-tip pens

Fountain pens

Cartoons are usually printed fairly small, but it is often easier for the cartoonist to draw them at a larger size. They can be reduced by computer for printing.

The cartoonist is told what the printed size will be. By drawing a diagonal line across a box that size, he or she can extend the box so that it is larger but still the same shape.

Cartoonist's drawing size

Diagonal line drawn across picture size

Printed size of picture

Go to **www.usborne-quicklinks.com** for a link to a Web site where you can see how a professional cartoonist uses watercolor pencils.

Short comic strips

A comic strip is like a joke told in more than one frame. As in a single cartoon, the joke needs to be visual. It can be like a short story with a punchline.

In comic strips, it can be hard to make characters look the same in each frame. To start with, only use one or two characters. Give them features that are easy to draw.

How to start

Close-ups varied with larger scenes

As with single cartoons, think of a theme first and make up a joke around it.

Divide the joke up into three or four stages. You can vary the sizes of the frames, and vary

close-ups with larger scenes, to make the strip look more interesting.

Speech bubbles

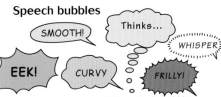

Put bubbles over background areas with no detail.

You can put speech and thoughts in bubbles in the pictures. These can be different shapes. The shape of a bubble may suggest the way something is being said.

Keep the speech short or the strip gets complicated and the bubbles take up too much room. Make sure you allow room for bubbles when you sketch out the pictures.

Pencil lines

It is best to do the lettering before you draw the bubble outline. Use a pen with a fine tip.

To get the letters the same height, draw parallel pencil lines and write the letters evenly

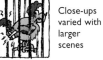

in between them, as above. Then erase the pencil lines. The letters are likely to be fairly small, so it is best to use capital letters which are easier to read.

A finished comic strip

This strip is about a caveman and a dinosaur. The caveman is a fairly easy character to repeat from frame to frame because of his simple features and clothing.

Speech bubble over the sky area

Different sized frames make strip more interesting

Sound effects make the strip more fun. As you read it you imagine the noises, so it is a little like watching a film.

Bright colors make the characters stand out. The background is paler.

A lot of the humor in a comic strip comes from the expressions on the characters' faces.

When positioning speech bubbles, remember that people read from left to right down the frame. They will read bubbles at the top before they read bubbles further down.

Borders for the strip

The borders around the frames can make a strip look neat and tidy or free and artistic. Here are some ideas for different borders you can try.

Freehand borders give a sketchy effect. To keep them straight, draw the lines in pencil with a ruler. Then go over them freehand in ink.

Paintbrush borders look good because the line varies slightly in thickness. You can get a straight line by using the method below.

Border around strip

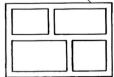

Use a ruler and a pen with a slightly thicker tip than the one you used for the lettering. You can put the whole strip in a larger box.

Freehand borders are finished off without a ruler.

1. Place a ruler just below where you want to draw the line.
2. Hold the ruler down and run your fingers along it as you paint. (You may need to practice this.)

17

Long comic strips

You may have your own favorite comics. The stories in them are fun and easy to read because there is very little text and a lot of action in the pictures.

Creating a comic strip

A practical joke... an escape from the zoo... an Arctic expedition... a kidnapping!

The first thing to do when creating a comic strip is to think of a plot. It needs to be funny or dramatic – or both! The plot needs an exciting finish.

Bad-tempered

Tough and reliable

Lively and clever

Grumbling and lazy

The characters need strong personalities which will come across in the pictures. You can tell what the characters above are like just by looking at them.

Find out how to use special effects to add excitement to your pictures on pages 20-21.

The plot needs to be full of action to keep the reader interested. The story needs to move fast and something new must happen in each picture.

These two pages describe how a cartoon artist creates a comic strip to tell a story. Try making up your own comic strip in the same way.

Writing a script

A script explains what is happening in each frame of the comic strip. It describes the scenery, what the characters are doing and saying and any sound effects. Some artists write their own scripts. Others illustrate scripts written by someone else.

The page of a comic is a fixed size so the story needs to be divided up into the right number of frames to fit on it.

```
SCRIPT: THE TESTTUBE AFFAIR
PAGE 1

Frame 1.
Scene: Room furnished with an iron
bedstead. There is a small window.
Terry is sitting tied to a chair,
busy freeing himself.

Thought bubble: Whoever heard of a
kidnapper who couldn't tie knots?
I've been lucky.

Frame 2.
Scene: Sparsely-furnished room.
There is a radio on the table. Two
mean and grubby-looking kidnappers
sit playing cards.

First kidnapper: Why do we always
get the boring jobs?
Second kidnapper: Shuddup and listen!

Frame 3.
Close-up of radio blaring...
```

Drawing the strip

Here you can see how the script on the left (you can only see the first page) was made into a finished comic strip. It was drawn using a dip pen with a sprung nib. The nib gives a varying thickness of line depending on how hard it is pressed.

The story is mainly told in the pictures, but there are bubbles for speech and thoughts.

Some frames can be left without borders to add variety.

Light pressure on the nib gives a finer line.

Pressure on the nib gives a thick line.

Sound effects can help to tell the story.

Frame sizes are varied to make strip more interesting.

Scenery can make the strip come to life.

A line of text at the top can explain changes of scene or time lapses.

19

Special effects

Special effects can make cartoons look exciting. Here are some ideas for how to add drama and atmosphere to your pictures.

You can make them spooky, mysterious, shocking or scary. You can also find out how to add sound effects.

Sound effects

You can add sound effects by using words and shapes which suggest the sound. The most common ones are explosions, but there are lots of others you can use.

Jagged speech bubble suggests shock

WAH!

TWEET! TWEET!

CRASH!

CREAK

BOOM!

Shadows and silhouettes

Using different lighting effects for night pictures can make them look creepy or mysterious. Here are some suggestions:

Huge shadow on wall

Silhouette of a castle in a thunderstorm

Silhouettes in a lighted window. These are made by people sitting in front of a source of light.

20

Scary effects

This picture uses the effect of a harmless tree that looks scary in the dark. You could try a similar picture using a hat and coat hanging up to look like a sinister person.

Lines suggesting speed

This type of shading, where you use lots of lines close together, is called hatching.

Two comic strips

These comic strips use some of the special effects described on these pages.

1

2

A comic strip to try

Here is a script for a comic strip involving special effects for you to try:

Frame 1. Silhouettes of people by a bonfire.
Frame 2. Boy dressed up as a ghost frightens them away.

Frame 3. Boy takes sheet off and is shocked to hear laughter coming from a spooky tree silhouette.
Sound effect: HO HO HO

Drawing animals

You can draw animals in a similar way to drawing people, by using simple shapes and lines and adding features.

Animals make good cartoons because you can use their natural characteristics, such as claws, tails, ears and so on to give them personality. Here are lots of animals to draw.

Cat

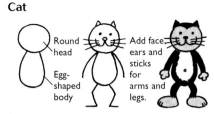

Round head

Egg-shaped body

Add face, ears and sticks for arms and legs.

Dog

Floppy ears

Wagging tail

Head slightly pointed at top

Mouse

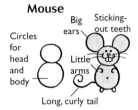

Big ears

Sticking-out teeth

Circles for head and body

Little arms

Long, curly tail

Bird

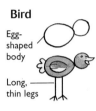

Egg-shaped body

Long, thin legs

Pig

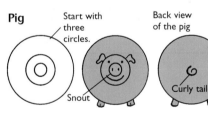

Start with three circles.

Back view of the pig

Snout

Curly tail

Giraffe

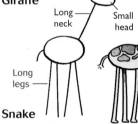

Long neck

Small head

Goofy expression

Long legs

Add small ears and horns.

Elephant

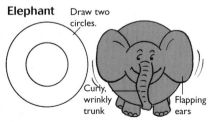

Draw two circles.

Curly, wrinkly trunk

Flapping ears

Snake

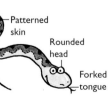

Draw a wiggly shape.

Patterned skin

Rounded head

Forked tongue

Internet links

For more information about drawing cartoons, go to the Usborne Quicklinks Web site at **www.usborne-quicklinks.com** and click on the number of the Web site you want to visit.

Web site 1 At this site you'll find step-by-step instructions to help you draw and color a dozen different cartoons, from penguins and puppies to rabbits and cats.

Web site 2 Here you'll find step-by-step instructions for how to draw cartoon characters and animals. Click on a cartoon to find out how to draw it.

Web site 3 At this site there are lots of cartoon tutorials. You can also have drawing tips e-mailed to you each week.

Web site 4 Find out how to draw lots of different cartoons, from wild animals to fantasy figures.

Web site 5 See some fun ideas that show you how to draw cartoon faces using numbers and letters.

Web site 6 At this Web site you'll see how a few lines can turn into all kinds of things, with a little imagination.

Web site 7 At this site you'll find links to lots of Web sites for famous cartoon characters.

Web site 8 People have been telling stories in pictures for thousands of years. This site shows examples from cave paintings to Spiderman.

Web site 9 If you are interested in animated cartoons, you can go behind the scenes and find out all about how they are created from start to finish on this Web site.

Web site 10 Go on a virtual tour of the Hanna-Barbera studios, where many famous cartoons were created.

Web site 11 Here you'll find some useful tips and advice to help you experiment and practice your drawing.

Web site 12 This site offers useful tips, including advice on what you can do if you want to have your cartoons published.

Web site 13 How are different colors made? Learn all about the world of color on this fun Web site.

HOW TO DRAW

Dinosaurs

Marit Claridge

Designed by Mike Pringle and Richard Johnson
Illustrated by Val Biro, Philip Hood and John Shackell

Edited by Judy Tatchell

Consultant: John Shackell

CONTENTS

26 Drawing dinosaurs
28 Shapes and colors
30 Heads and tails
32 A vegetarian giant
34 Sea monsters
36 Flying creatures
38 Dinosaur characters
40 Cave people
42 Dinosaur comic strips
44 Cartoon lettering
45 Moving pictures
46 Dinosaur stencils
47 Internet links

Drawing dinosaurs

Millions of years ago, monstrous dinosaurs and other strange animals ruled the Earth. They are fun to draw because, although there are some clues as to what they looked like, nobody can be exactly sure and you can use your imagination.

Drawing around skeletons

Dinosaurs died out millions of years before humans appeared. The only clues to how they looked come from parts of their skeletons which have been found preserved in rock. These remains are called fossils. People called paleontologists piece the fossils together, figuring out how the missing bits of skeleton might have looked.

Look for pictures of dinosaur skeletons, which you can trace around as shown here. Remember to leave space for the missing muscles and flesh.

Small bones are supported by small muscles, so the outline is close to the bone here.

Big bones need strong muscles to support them, so leave plenty of space for muscle here.

Coloring dinosaurs

Nobody knows exactly what colors the dinosaurs were. Most were probably fairly similar to the trees and ferns around them.

Paleontologists base their color guesses on the reptiles and plants alive today. You, however, can color them as brightly as you like.

Drawing styles

In this part of the book you can find out how to draw realistic-looking prehistoric animals as well as cartoon dinosaurs.

You can also find out how to draw cartoon cave people.

Dinosaurs and cave people often appear together in cartoons, even though dinosaurs died out long before cave people appeared.

Scaling up

You can learn a lot about how to draw prehistoric life by copying the illustrations in this section. If you want to make your drawing bigger than the one in the book, you can scale up the illustration using a grid.

Draw a grid on tracing paper made up of equal-sized squares.

Put the grid over the picture you want to copy.

Draw another light pencil grid on your drawing paper. To double the size of the picture, draw the same number of squares but twice the size of those on the tracing grid.

Look at the squares laid on top of the picture. Copy the shapes in each one into the same square on the drawing paper grid.

Erase the grid lines when you have inked the outline.

Shapes and colors

On these two pages there are tips on how to draw and color prehistoric animals.

You may find these techniques useful later in this part of the book.

Simple shapes

Prehistoric deer

1 **2** **3**

However complicated an animal looks, it is made up of simpler shapes. Throughout this part of the book there are line drawings which show how to

build up the animals using simple shapes. Draw the red lines first, then draw the blue and then the green.

Colors

Many of the animals in this section are colored using watercolor paints. Some of the colors have unusual names. These are explained in **Artist's colors** boxes.

A paintbox with a large range of colors should have all the colors you need. You can also buy tubes of watercolors in any color you wish.

Artist's colors

Ochre is a pale brownish-yellow.

Washes

A wash is a thin coat of watery paint. When you color a large animal, mix up plenty of the wash color in a separate container.

Skin textures

Dinosaurs had thick, leathery skins like elephants, or dry, bumpy skins. You can use the tips below to paint and crayon the skins of the dinosaurs in this section.

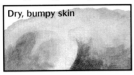

Dry, bumpy skin

1. Color the area with a light to medium wash. When it is dry, add a second, darker layer to the shaded areas.

2. Cover the area with thick, white spots. Mix some wash color with the white to darken the spots in the shaded areas.

3. Add dark shadows beneath the spots and draw extra dark lines beneath the body to strengthen the shadows.

Using a sponge

For another bumpy skin, begin with a wash, as before. Then dip a small sponge in a darker mix of paint and dab it gently over the area.

Thick, leathery skin

Begin with a background wash. When it is dry, draw dark, heavy lines where the body creases. Finally add highlights with dry, white paint.

or

With crayons and pencils, color the dinosaur with the paper resting on a rough surface, such as sandpaper, cement or grainy wood.

Artist's tip

Some of the prehistoric creatures in this part of the book are two-legged. A common problem when drawing them is that they can look off balance. This makes them appear weak.

To make them balance, there must be as much weight in front of the legs as behind. Draw a vertical line and build your animal up around it.

Weight too far back

Weight too far forward

Draw equal amounts of the animal's bulk on either side of the line.

Line shows where the animal's weight is falling.

Heads and tails

The dinosaurs on these two pages have strange heads or tails and odd bodies.

These make them fun to draw and ideal for turning into cartoons.

Stegosaurus

Use a darker shade for the far plates and legs. This makes them look further away.

Plates

The head hangs low, as the front legs are shorter than the back legs.

Sketch the basic shape of the Stegosaurus (say Steg-oh-saw-rus) in pencil. Begin with the body, then add the neck, head, tail and legs. Draw the

plates last. To color the Stegosaurus, use the techniques shown on page 29 for dry, bumpy skin on the body and thick, leathery skin on the legs.

Ankylosaurus

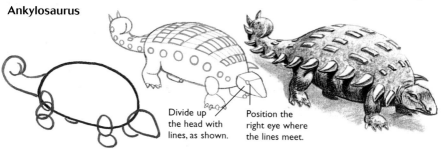

Divide up the head with lines, as shown.

Position the right eye where the lines meet.

Above are the basic shapes for a plant-eating dinosaur called an Ankylosaurus (say An-kee-lo-saw-rus).

Draw faint circles along the body to position the body spikes and curved lines to position the back plates.

Add spikes and back plates. Leave white highlights on them. Add strong shadows under the spikes and body.

30

Crested dinosaurs

Some dinosaurs had crests on their heads which probably helped them recognize each other. The crests had air passages inside, which meant the dinosaurs could make loud, bellowing calls. The crests may have been very colorful.

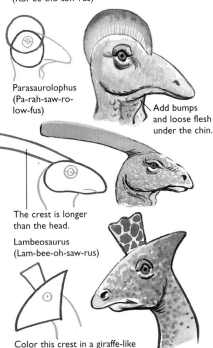

Corythosaurus
(Kor-ee-tho-saw-rus)

Parasaurolophus
(Pa-rah-saw-ro-low-fus)

Add bumps and loose flesh under the chin.

The crest is longer than the head.

Lambeosaurus
(Lam-bee-oh-saw-rus)

Color this crest in a giraffe-like fashion, using vivid colored patches.

Cartoon dinosaurs

The Ankylosaurus used the bone at the end of its tail to fend off meat-eaters. Try copying this cartoon, which makes fun of the situation.

Curved lines indicate the direction of movement of the tail club.

Squinting eyes and trembling outline show pain.

These short lines repeat the shape of the club. They start faintly and get stronger toward the club.

The low eyelids give a lazy, unconcerned look.

Make your own monster

You could try mixing some of the heads, tails and bodies on these pages to make your own imaginary monster.

A vegetarian giant

The Diplodocus (Dip-lo-doh-kus) was the longest dinosaur. It measured almost 90ft from nose to tail – about as long as a tennis court.

Use a darker, thicker mix of the wash color for the shadows under the body.

Wrinkles

Draw in wrinkles around the legs and where the tail and neck bend.

Color the far legs a darker shade.

Shade under the body and neck and in the curve of the tail.

Draw the oval body shape first. Then add the long neck and tail and the heavy legs.

The Diplodocus had thick, leathery skin, like an elephant. Color it with shades of green watercolor, using the technique shown on page 29.

Turn your animal around

A simple clay model can be a great help if you want to draw your Diplodocus from different angles.

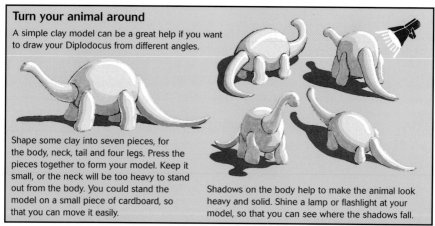

Shape some clay into seven pieces, for the body, neck, tail and four legs. Press the pieces together to form your model. Keep it small, or the neck will be too heavy to stand out from the body. You could stand the model on a small piece of cardboard, so that you can move it easily.

Shadows on the body help to make the animal look heavy and solid. Shine a lamp or flashlight at your model, so that you can see where the shadows fall.

In the swamp

The Diplodocus lived in swamps. Try drawing a wet, glossy Diplodocus in a prehistoric swamp.

Paint simple leaf shapes.

Less detail in distant trees

White highlights make the skin look wet.

Use darker shades below.

Steam rising

Let colors run together.

Keep near edges sharp.

Use muddy browns for the water. Add touches of blue to reflect the sky.

Get a swampy water effect by taking wiggly lines from roots and stems.

Draw the outline of the Diplodocus and tree trunks in pencil. Paint ferns and trees with plenty of creepers. Color the trees and water with very wet washes.

While the paint is still damp, dab some of the color away with tissue. This gives the effect of steam rising. Color the Diplodocus as on the page opposite.

A worm's eye view

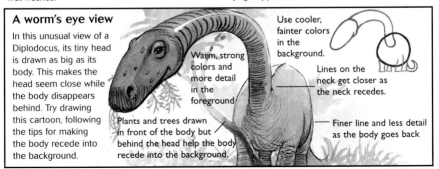

In this unusual view of a Diplodocus, its tiny head is drawn as big as its body. This makes the head seem close while the body disappears behind. Try drawing this cartoon, following the tips for making the body recede into the background.

Use cooler, fainter colors in the background.

Warm, strong colors and more detail in the foreground

Lines on the neck get closer as the neck recedes.

Finer line and less detail as the body goes back

Plants and trees drawn in front of the body but behind the head help the body recede into the background.

Go to **www.usborne-quicklinks.com** for a link to a Web site where you can see how a professional dinosaur artist created a realistic-looking prehistoric scene.

For an explosive sky, start at the top with red. Fade down to bright yellow. When dry, add white above the volcano. Splash on lots of red mixed with the volcano color for cloud and debris.

Artist's colors

Viridian is a deep turquoise.

The blurred outline suggests movement.

Add some of the volcano color to the sea to look like reflections.

For splashes, paint over the sea and rocks with a thick viridian and white mix. Add pure white around the edges and shooting away from the middle of the splash.

Color rocks with a pale greenish-gray wash. When dry, use a sponge to dab on dark bluish-gray or green paint.

When the sea is dry, add thin white wavy movement lines and small circles and blobs for bubbles.

Add splashes of pink and orange on the rocks for coral. Allow some of the colors to blend together.

Mosasaur
(Mose-a-sor)

Under the sea

First color the monsters, the coral and underwater rocks. Leave these to dry. Then cover the whole area with a viridian wash (don't make it too wet or the colors will run). When this dries, add wavy lines of darker viridian across the picture. Paint darker viridian lines alongside the Mosasaur. These help to make the creature look as if it is moving through the sea.

Flying creatures

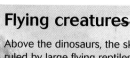

Above the dinosaurs, the skies were ruled by large flying reptiles, called pterosaurs. Here you can find out how to draw two different types, as well as a strip cartoon about an Archaeopteryx, the first real bird.

Paint the Pteranodon (Ter-rah-no-don) with a thin, gray wash. When it is dry, go over it again with a thin, pinkish-brown wash.

Pteranodon

Draw a faint dotted line and use this to position the body, legs and arms. Add the wings, neck and head.

Add shadows and veins in dark brown.

Use a thick mix of the pinkish-brown color for highlights.

Follow the tips on pages 34 and 35 for coloring the sea and rocks.

Artist's tip

You can save time by using a hairdryer to dry the wash.

Archaeopteryx

The Archaeopteryx (Ar-kee-op-ter-iks) used its sharp claws to climb trees and its wings to glide. It was too heavy to fly and its beak full of teeth would have made it nose-heavy.

Try copying this strip cartoon about an Archaeopteryx.

Beads of sweat show effort.

Draw the outline and feathers with a black felt-tip. Color the bird with bright colored pencils or felt-tips.

Wide eyes, curved brows and gaping mouth suggest mounting panic.

Bird's eye view

Animals and trees look quite different from above. The parts of the body that are nearer to you look bigger than those that are further away.

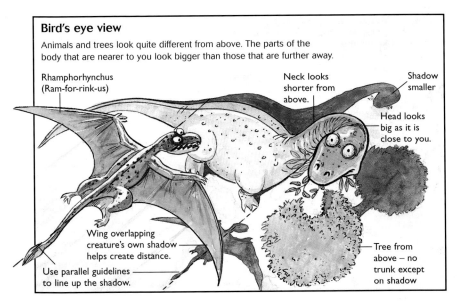

Rhamphorhynchus
(Ram-for-rink-us)

Neck looks shorter from above.

Shadow smaller

Head looks big as it is close to you.

Wing overlapping creature's own shadow helps create distance.

Use parallel guidelines to line up the shadow.

Tree from above – no trunk except on shadow

Lines show the direction of movement.

CRUNCH

Radiating lines make the impact look more dramatic.

Extra beads of sweat suggest greater effort as Archaeopteryx climbs the tree again.

Dinosaur characters

People like to write stories about dinosaurs and prehistoric times because of the excitement of the unknown. All that remains of these creatures are their skeletons, and the rest has to be made up. This mixture of reality and fantasy makes them ideal subjects for stories.

The dinosaurs shown here are drawn in a cartoon story-book style. They are given characters, like people in a story.

Tyrannosaurus rex

The Tyrannosaurus rex (Tie-ran-oh-saw-rus rex), or T. rex, was one of the biggest meat-eaters that ever lived. Its head alone was five feet long – big enough to swallow a man whole. Try painting the fierce T. rex below using a masking fluid* to give its colorful skin a bumpy texture. You can also use this technique for the Triceratops on page 39, and on other dinosaurs with scaly skin.

Dot masking fluid on the back.

Masking fluid lines on stomach and tail

1. Copy or trace the T. rex. Dip the end of a paper clip in masking fluid and paint as shown – do not use a brush or you will ruin it.

Green for back

Yellow and orange for stomach

2. When the masking fluid is dry, color the T. rex in with watercolor.

White marks left behind by fluid.

3. Once the paint is dry, rub off the masking fluid with your fingers. This will leave white marks.

Paint over the whole dinosaur with light washes of different colors to make colorful skin marks.

*You can buy masking fluid from art supply stores.

Triceratops

This brave, charging Triceratops (Try-ser-a-tops) was a fierce, plant-eating dinosaur. Its huge, frilled head, three horns, frowning eyes and strange, beaked mouth help to give it a lot of character. Trace or copy the Triceratops here. Use masking fluid for texture and color it with orange, yellow, green and brown watercolor.

Add extra, detailed markings with dark colored pencils.

A timid T. rex

In most pictures the T. rex is shown as terrible and frightening. This T. rex is given a timid character.

It looks alarmed – as it may have been if charged by the heavily-armored Triceratops.

Here it is, running away. The staring eyes, slightly opened mouth and turned head make it look even more alarmed than before.

The downturned mouth and backward-looking eyes give the T. rex a worried expression.

Cave people

On these two pages you can see how to draw a family of cave people.

Caveman and woman

Use the same basic shape for both the caveman and cavewoman.

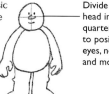

Divide head into quarters to position eyes, nose and mouth.

Draw clothes, hair and beard outlines with a fine felt-tip.

Color the clothes with yellow felt-tip pen. Use a brown felt-tip pen for the spots.

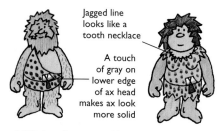

Jagged line looks like a tooth necklace

A touch of gray on lower edge of ax head makes ax look more solid

Add hair on his arms and legs with a pencil.

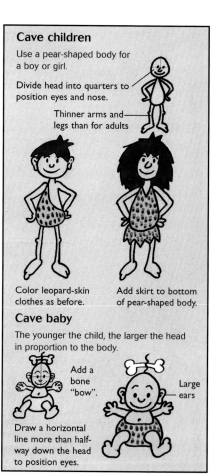

Cave children

Use a pear-shaped body for a boy or girl.

Divide head into quarters to position eyes and nose.

Thinner arms and legs than for adults

Color leopard-skin clothes as before.

Add skirt to bottom of pear-shaped body.

Cave baby

The younger the child, the larger the head in proportion to the body.

Add a bone "bow".

Large ears

Draw a horizontal line more than half-way down the head to position eyes.

40

Turning around

You can use the same basic body shapes to draw the cave children and adults from the front, back and side.

For a back view, turn feet away and fill head completely with hair color.

For a three-quarter view, move facial features to left or right. Add the nose in profile. Change the arms and legs as shown.

THAT'S MY MOM'S COAT HE'S WEARING!

GULP!

The side-on caveman in the cartoon above is drawn starting with the same body shape as for a front view. You only have to alter the arm and leg positions and draw the face in profile.

Here you can see how coloring just the relevant part of the picture makes the point of the joke stand out.

Cave family at home

This cartoon shows some tricks you can use to make your pictures more lively.

This boy's leg breaks out of the frame to give the impression of running into the picture.

For the blotchy effect, apply the paint with a sponge. Add more paint with a brush in darker areas.

WOOLY RHINO   DEER   THE NEIGHBORS

PTERRY

Lines repeat tail shape.

Clouds of dust help to show speed.

Dust where ball bounces

Dinosaur comic strips

A comic strip is a funny story told in more than one picture. Each picture is drawn within a frame, with speech and thought added in bubbles.

Try to make your characters look the same in each frame. It helps if you give them distinct features, such as a big nose or beard.

Artist's tip

You can turn the characters of your comic strip around with the help of tracing paper. This works for side views and three-quarter views. Trace the figure and simply turn the tracing over for the opposite view.

The tracing is like a mirror image where everything is reversed. If your character has clothes off one shoulder or a club in one hand, this has to be reversed back again.

Speech bubbles

You can add speech and thought bubbles to your story. Use capital letters and keep the speech short. You can also add sound effects, which you can find out about on page 44.

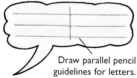

Draw parallel pencil guidelines for letters.

To center the lettering, draw a vertical line. Then put around the same number of letters on each side (count the spaces between words as one letter).

MAKE SURE THAT THE ARROW FROM THE SPEECH BUBBLE POINTS TO THE HEAD.

Pardon?

WHAT NOW?

With more than one speech bubble in a frame, people will read them from the top left corner down to the bottom right corner. Make sure you place them in the order you want them read.

Use small lettering in a large bubble for quiet speech.

For loud speech, do the opposite -

SPEAK UP!

A line of small circles from the bubble indicates thought.

1st 2nd 3rd 4th

Framing

Use the tips below to vary the size and shape of the picture frames. This makes the strip look more interesting.

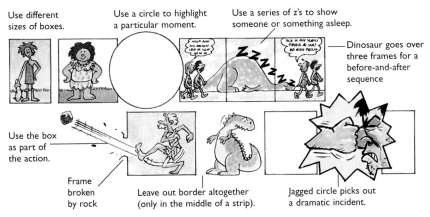

Use different sizes of boxes.

Use a circle to highlight a particular moment.

Use a series of z's to show someone or something asleep.

Dinosaur goes over three frames for a before-and-after sequence

Use the box as part of the action.

Frame broken by rock

Leave out border altogether (only in the middle of a strip).

Jagged circle picks out a dramatic incident.

A finished strip

This comic strip uses some of the techniques described. There are also some more tips for you to follow.

Flash breaking out of frame gives a dramatic effect

Add extra letters for a long scream.

Hint of smoke leads to next frame

Movement lines indicate head turning quickly

Circle broken by elbow

A close-up varies the look of the pictures.

Different sized frames

Action continues beyond the last frame

43

Cartoon lettering

You can make dramatic sound effects for your cartoons. Use colors and shapes that suggest the sound you want to make.

Try drawing the words on this page and then make up some words and shapes of your own.

The wiggly outlines of the letters make them look as if they have been squashed by the dinosaur's tail.

Draw soft, squishy letter shapes.

Extra letters give the impression of a long noise. The letters get bigger and bigger to suggest a loud growl.

Drop shadows

You can make the sound have more impact by adding a drop shadow. Use sharp letter angles to suggest a loud sound.

Draw the letter outlines, then trace them on to tracing paper. Use the tracing to draw the shadow under and to the right of the original.

Black in the shadow. You can also try using colored letters and shadows.

Extra dimensions

In this example, the word radiates out from the crashing caveman. This helps to give a three-dimensional effect.

Draw the caveman. Mark a point in the centre of his body and draw pencil guidelines radiating out from this point.

Use guidelines to draw the letters.

Add impact lines last.

Moving pictures

For fast-action cartoons there are simple ways to make your characters look as if they are on the run.

The two main ways to draw fast-running legs are shown in the cartoon below.

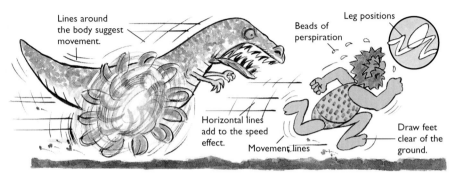

Lines around the body suggest movement.

Horizontal lines add to the speed effect.

Beads of perspiration

Leg positions

Movement lines

Draw feet clear of the ground.

The dinosaur's legs are a blurred spiral of lines. The foot shape is repeated again and again around the edge.

The caveman's legs have movement lines to show that he is running. In both methods the feet are clear of the ground.

Movement and distance

Add giant prehistoric ferns. Draw them large in the foreground and smaller as you go into the distance.

Draw figures in the foreground larger than those further away.

Fade the sky color toward the horizon.

Dust disappears

Here, dust kicked up by the runners helps to give the impression of movement. Draw the dust

clouds smaller as they disappear out of view to give depth to the cartoon.

Dinosaur stencils

You can make dinosaur stencils from thin cardboard – an empty cereal box will do. Carefully cut out the animal shape, so that you can use both the positive and the negative. The simpler the shape, the easier it is to cut out. Use a pair of small, sharp scissors.

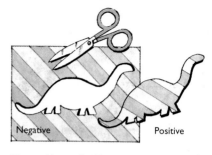

Negative

Positive

Candle wax textures

Candle wax resists paint and leaves interesting patterns. Use thin, white birthday candles.

You could copy the Diplodocus shape below to make a stencil.

Paint from side to center.

Hold down the negative stencil and paint over it with a yellow wash. Use a fairly dry wash.

When it is completely dry, draw wrinkles and scaly patterns over the Diplodocus with a candle.

Keep the stencil in place and paint all over the shape with a dark bluish-gray wash.

Paint plant silhouettes in a pale mauve wash. When dry, draw on stem and leaf shapes in candle wax. Finish with a dark mauve wash on top.

For this sky, paint the sun and then cover it with wax. Draw lines and swirls in wax for clouds. Paint over the top with a pink wash fading to yellow.

Apply lines of wax before adding the watercolor, to look like reflections.

Artist's tip
Cover the dinosaur with the positive stencil when you color the background. This keeps the shape clean.

Internet links

For more information about dinosaurs and how to draw them, go to the Usborne Quicklinks Web site at **www.usborne-quicklinks.com** and click on the number of the Web site you want to visit.

Web site 1 This Web site has lots of information on discovering dinosaurs, including an excellent step-by-step guide to drawing them.

Web site 2 You'll find over fifty detailed black-and-white drawings of dinosaurs and prehistoric mammals here. See how the artist uses shading to show different skin textures.

Web site 3 At this site you'll find links to hundreds of Web sites with color illustrations of all kinds of dinosaurs, to help you with dinosaur shapes, colors and textures.

Web site 4 This site has detailed pictures of dinosaurs and other creatures from different prehistoric periods. You can get some good ideas for drawing backgrounds for your pictures here.

Web site 5 Explore a vivid account of the last days of the dinosaurs, with some super-realistic illustrations.

Web site 6 Find out what it's like to walk with dinosaurs on this site, which brings many prehistoric creatures to life.

Web site 7 If you want to find out more about dinosaurs in general, or about a particular kind of dinosaur, you'll find a huge amount of information on this site.

Web site 8 Read all about recent spectacular dinosaur discoveries on this fascinating Web site.

Web site 9 Print out and color these dinosaur shapes to make 3-D dinosaur models, then try making your own.

Web site 10 Here, you'll find lots of ideas for drawing or coloring dinosaurs, and for making dinosaur models from wire or papier mâché.

Web site 11 Watch a short movie about the world of dinosaurs, and then try the quiz to test your dinosaur knowledge. You'll need a set of speakers or headphones to listen to the movie.

Web site 12 At this site there are six fun cartoon dinosaurs to draw, including a slobbery stegosaurus and a dino-baby. Click on one for step-by-step instructions.

HOW TO DRAW
MONSTERS

Cheryl Evans

Designed and illustrated by Graham Round
and Kim Blundell

Additional design and illustration by Brian Robertson

CONTENTS

50 About monsters
51 Getting ideas
52 Prehistoric monsters
54 Spooky monsters
56 Space aliens
58 Sea monsters
60 Man-made monsters
62 Dragons

64 Giants, ogres and trolls
66 Goblins, dwarfs and
   human horrors
68 Techniques and
   materials
70 People or monsters?
71 Internet links

About monsters

Monsters come in all shapes and sizes. They can be simple to draw or fairly tricky – you can make them as basic or as detailed as you like. This section shows you how to draw lots of different monsters and color them to make them look really dramatic.

Monster shapes

Made-up monster shape

You can draw traditional monsters or invent your own using all kinds of shapes.

Dragon

Dinosaur

Famous monsters

King Kong

Monsters are popular subjects for books, comics, cartoons and movies. How many famous monsters can you name?

Vac-dragon

All kinds of monsters

There are lots of different monsters in this section. For example, there are dinosaurs on pages 52-53 and aliens on pages 56-57.

Fuzzy alien

Unusual monsters

You can turn anything into a monster. Try a vacuum cleaner (page 60) or a fuzzy alien (page 57).

Scary settings

Scenery can make your monsters more exciting. See how to do a watery background for sea monsters on page 59, or a spooky graveyard on page 55, for instance.

Things to use

In this part of the book you will be using pencils, felt-tip pens, wax crayons, chalk and lots of other materials. There is a chart on pages 64-65 to remind you of all the different things you can do.

Getting ideas

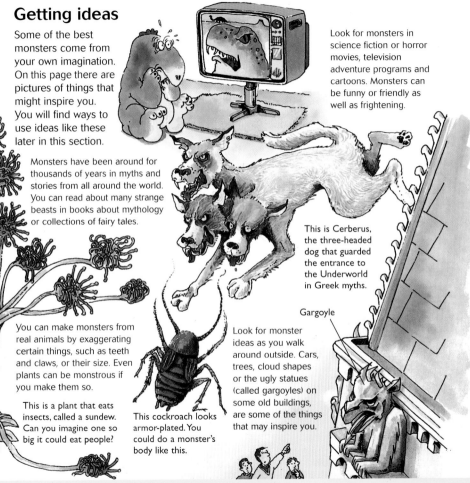

Some of the best monsters come from your own imagination. On this page there are pictures of things that might inspire you. You will find ways to use ideas like these later in this section.

Monsters have been around for thousands of years in myths and stories from all around the world. You can read about many strange beasts in books about mythology or collections of fairy tales.

Look for monsters in science fiction or horror movies, television adventure programs and cartoons. Monsters can be funny or friendly as well as frightening.

This is Cerberus, the three-headed dog that guarded the entrance to the Underworld in Greek myths.

Gargoyle

You can make monsters from real animals by exaggerating certain things, such as teeth and claws, or their size. Even plants can be monstrous if you make them so.

This is a plant that eats insects, called a sundew. Can you imagine one so big it could eat people?

This cockroach looks armor-plated. You could do a monster's body like this.

Look for monster ideas as you walk around outside. Cars, trees, cloud shapes or the ugly statues (called gargoyles) on some old buildings, are some of the things that may inspire you.

Go to *www.usborne-quicklinks.com* for a link to a Web site where you can see some of the great gargoyles to be found around New York City.

Prehistoric monsters

Dinosaurs were huge, real-life monsters that existed on Earth 65 to 225 million years ago. Here you can find out how to draw and color some cartoon dinosaurs. You can adapt these basic shapes to make many others.

Tyrannosaurus rex

Tyrannosaurus rex was the king of the meat-eating dinosaurs. It could grow to nearly 49 feet long. The box below shows you how to draw it. Hints for coloring and other details are shown on the right.

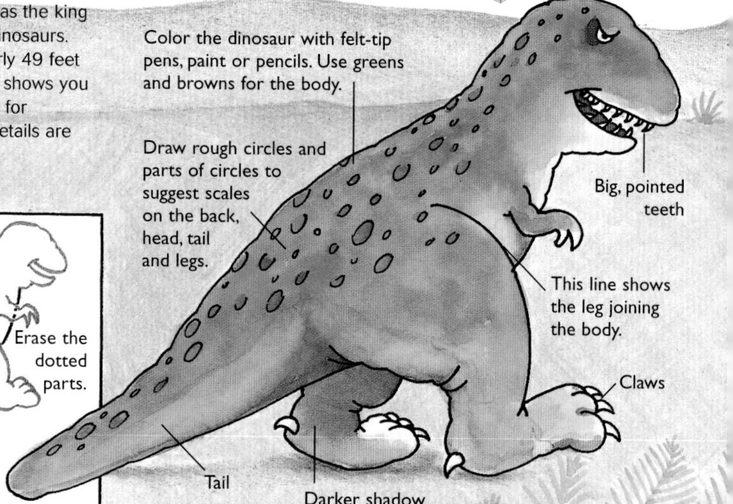

Color the dinosaur with felt-tip pens, paint or pencils. Use greens and browns for the body.

Draw rough circles and parts of circles to suggest scales on the back, head, tail and legs.

Big, pointed teeth

This line shows the leg joining the body.

Claws

Drawing the shape

Erase the dotted parts.

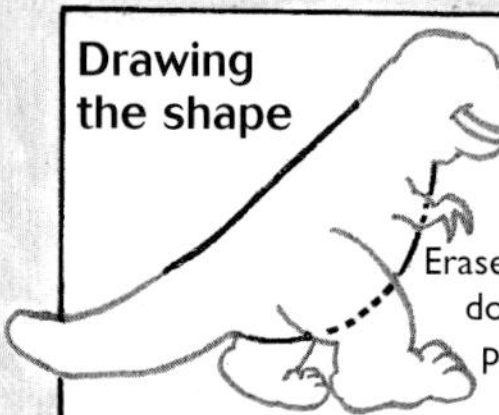

Use a pencil to copy the lines shown in the picture in this order:

— First the black lines
— Next the orange lines
— Then the blue lines

The boxes on page 53 show you how to draw two more dinosaurs. Copy the lines in the same order – black, then orange, then blue.

Tail

Darker shadow underneath body

Giant fern

During the dinosaur period, the Earth was warm and covered in dense forests. Plants were giant-sized, though many of them were like forest plants today.

Try drawing giant ferns, like this one, as a setting for your dinosaurs. Do curved lines for stems. Add narrow leaves on each side. The leaves get shorter toward the tip of each stem.

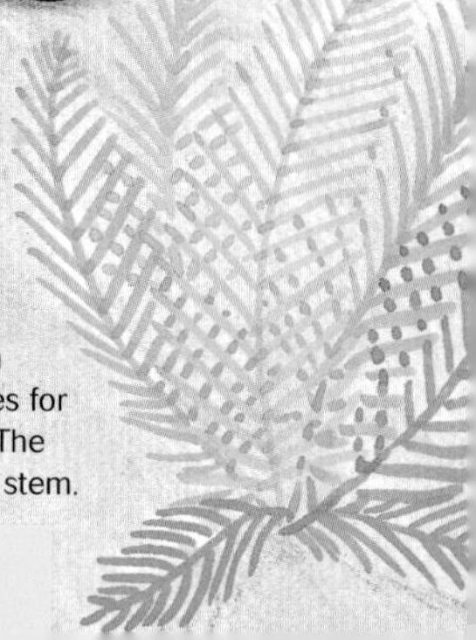

Go to **www.usborne-quicklinks.com** for a link to a Web site where you will find a huge dinosaur picture gallery.

Flying monsters

At the same time as the dinosaurs, there were also flying reptiles, like this Pterodactyl. Copy the lines in the box below to draw it.

The Pterodactyl has a scaly body like Tyrannosaurus rex. Use brown paint or felt-tip.

Use colored pencils for the wings (see below). This contrasts well with the body.

Sharp teeth

Add the wings last.

Wing texture

The Pterodactyl has bat-like wings. Get this effect by putting a leaf face-down under the paper and rubbing over it with a brown pencil.

Use a leaf with veins that stick out. A horse-chestnut or maple is good.

Diplodocus

This is a Diplodocus. See how to draw it in the box below.

You can use the Diplodocus shape, or any of the shapes on this page, as a base for drawing other monsters.

Use grays for the Diplodocus.

Add an eye and a mouth.

Go over darker parts twice.

Put a dark shadow underneath the body.

Diplodocus skin

To get a wrinkly skin texture, as in this picture, put a sheet of rough sandpaper under your drawing and color over the top with wax crayons or colored pencils. Press fairly hard.

53

Spooky monsters

Ghosts are scary because nobody knows exactly what they are or if they even exist. Some people say they are shadowy, almost see-through shapes that appear in the darkness. Here are some different kinds for you to try.

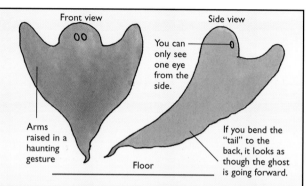

Floating ghost

This floating ghost shape looks a little like someone with a sheet over their head and their arms raised.

Give it a rounded head and wiggly "tail" where its feet would be, so it looks as though it is fading away.

Draw the floor below the "tail", so that the ghost seems to float.

Front view

Side view

You can only see one eye from the side.

Arms raised in a haunting gesture

Floor

If you bend the "tail" to the back, it looks as though the ghost is going forward.

Changing the shape

You can change the shape of a ghost to make it do different things. Give it an expression, too. Try some of the ideas below.

Make a ghost do something normal, like sitting and reading. You can see the chair through the ghost.

A furious ghost has hands on its hips and an angry face. Do frowning eyebrows and a straight line for a mouth. Red is a good angry color.

Ghostly colors

Here's a good way to do ghostly colors: draw the ghost outline with a felt-tip pen. Then smudge the line with a wet paintbrush and spread the color inside the shape.

Expressions to try

Why not try some ghostly expressions? Here are some tips to help you.

Friendly: round eyes, curved eyebrows and a smile

Surprised: open mouth, round eyes, raised eyebrows

Sad: eyebrows and eyes slope, mouth curves down

Graveyard phantom

Follow these stages to draw the spooky phantom in an eerie graveyard on the right. It is easier to do than it may look.

1. Make a charcoal patch on white paper with a charcoal pencil or stick.

2. With an eraser, erase a ghost shape, gravestones and blades of grass.

3. Add details with charcoal, as in the picture.

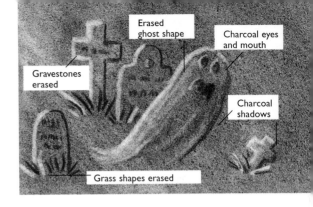

Erased ghost shape

Charcoal eyes and mouth

Gravestones erased

Charcoal shadows

Grass shapes erased

Headless specter

Here is another type of ghost. It is in historical costume and has its head under its arm. To draw one like it, use white chalk on black paper. The instructions should help.

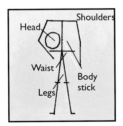

Shoulders

Head

Waist

Legs

Body stick

With a pencil, draw a stick man like this on your paper. Do legs twice as long as the body. Draw the head half as long as the body and to one side. Add lines for waist, shoulders and arms.

Join shoulders and waist. Do the neck ruff, bloomers and feet. Add details from the picture on the left. Erase extra lines. Go over the outline in chalk, then smudge it gently with your finger.*

*Stop further smudging with fixative spray (see page 68).

Space aliens

What do you think aliens from outer space look like? Are they like slightly odd-looking people, or are they completely different?

Here are some different kinds of aliens for you to try, and some space backgrounds for them too.

Little green Martian

1. To draw the Martian, start with rough pencil circles for his head, body and feet.

2 and 3. With your pencil, add the lines shown in red in these two pictures.

4. Erase any unwanted lines. Do the final outline in black and color him in.

Double space scene

Here's a way to get two dramatic space scenes at the same time. You need wax crayons, chalk pastels, a blunt pencil and two sheets of white paper. Just follow the steps below.

For these pictures you need three layers of color. Use chalk pastel for the first layer. Cover a sheet of paper with bright patches of chalk as shown here.

Color over the chalk with a bright wax crayon — orange or yellow, say. Do the third layer with a dark wax crayon such as blue or green. It will look a little like this.

Lay a second sheet of paper on top of the one you have colored. Draw stars, planets, spaceships or aliens in pencil on the top sheet. Press fairly hard.

56

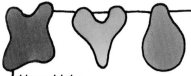

Moon blobs

Make blob aliens by drawing shapes like those above and adding features to them. You and your friends could draw blobs for each other to turn into aliens.

Do an outer space scene by drawing blob monsters on the moon. Paint the moon's mountains and craters white and gray and do a black sky with stars. A good way to spray stars is to dip an old toothbrush in white paint. Hold it bristles-down over the paper and run a finger along the bristles.

These blobs have been made into aliens in the scene below.

Crater

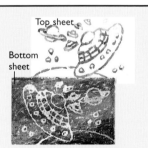

Top sheet

Bottom sheet

Remove the top sheet and turn it over. You now have two pictures. The one on the top sheet is made with wax crayon lifted from the other sheet by the pencil lines.

Friendly, fuzzy alien

This fuzzy alien looks soft and friendly. Use charcoal or a soft pencil to draw it. (Pencils can be hard or soft. Find out more about this on page 68.) This is what you do:

Draw a big nose.

Draw lines backward and forward like this.

Move in a circle around the nose.

Draw the fuzzy ball body as shown above, without taking your pencil off the paper except to avoid the nose.

Smudge the ball with your finger to make it look soft. Add eyes, legs and boots.

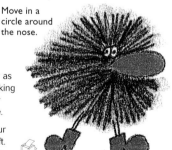

Go to **www.usborne-quicklinks.com** for a link to a Web site where you can learn how to draw all kinds of weird-looking aliens and spacecraft.

Sea monsters

These monsters are all based on things that live in the sea. Here you can find out how to draw them, color them and do a watery background.

Giant octopus

This giant octopus is spinning in a cloud of its own dark ink so you cannot see how big it is or where all its tentacles are. Perhaps one of them is reaching out to grab you!

You can see half a head and one evil red eye.

Tentacles twist and curl.

Suckers

Add white stripes.

How to draw it

Draw the whole octopus lightly in pencil. It has a blobby head and eight coiling tentacles.

Mix black and blue paint and splash it around the monster with a brush, hiding parts of it.

When the splashes dry, paint the parts of octopus that you can still see black. Add details as above.

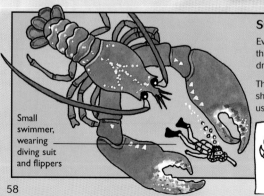

Small swimmer, wearing diving suit and flippers

Supersized sea creatures

Everyone knows that lobsters are smaller than people. But see what happens if you draw them the other way around, as here.

There are some more small sea creature shapes below. Try doing similar pictures using them.

Crab

Sea anemone

Fantastic fish

Invent a fantastic fish monster by drawing a big fish shape like this, with a huge mouth, sharp teeth, bulbous eyes and so on. Find out how to give it a slimy fish skin below.

Staring eyes

Spiky fins and tail

Sharp teeth

Sharp shapes look scary.

Slimy fish skin

To do a slimy fish skin, first paint your fish with water or very watery color. While it is still very wet, dab on blobs of bright paint. The blobs will smudge and blot to give spotted markings. Paint eyes and other details when the fish is dry.

Water wash

To do a water wash background as on this page, paint clean water all over your paper with a thick paintbrush. While it is still very wet, add watery blue and green paint in streaks. Let them mix and merge. Tape all four edges of the paper onto a flat surface while it dries to stop it from wrinkling.

Sea serpent

This sea serpent in the seaweed is colored with wax crayons. If you use crayons to draw an underwater scene, you can put a water wash (see right) over it afterward. Water and wax don't mix, so the crayon will show through.

Drawing the serpent

Draw a wiggly serpent shape in pencil. With wax crayon, add fronds of weeds. Make some go over the serpent's body and some go behind it. Color the serpent with wax crayons, except where the weeds go over its body.

59

Man-made monsters

If you can imagine things like a machine coming alive or a bad-tempered house, you can make monsters out of almost anything. Making something that is not alive look as though it can think or move is called anthropomorphism. See how to do it here.

Household horrors

Imagine household objects coming alive and doing things of their own accord. They may be nice, but you can make them horrible, like this stove and vacuum cleaner.

Crazy stove

In the box on the right is an ordinary stove shape. On the far side of it you can see one that has been made into a stove monster.

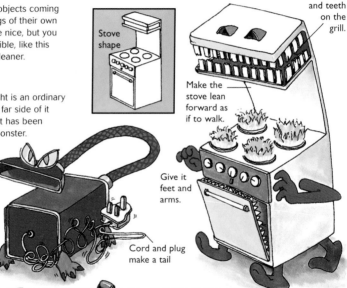

Stove shape

Put eyes and teeth on the grill.

Make the stove lean forward as if to walk.

Give it feet and arms.

Vac-dragon

This vacuum cleaner turns into a dragon with a snaky neck. The sucking part becomes a head with a wide mouth. Just add two evil eyes and feet with claws.

Cord and plug make a tail

Kitchen shapes

Scissors

Cheese grater

Egg whisk

Here are some kitchen shapes to turn into monsters. Copy them and add eyes, arms, legs and teeth as you like.

Dark doors look like open mouths.

Bottles on step look like teeth.

Reflections in windows make eyes.

Mean streets

On a dark night, in a badly-lit street, a row of houses can look menacing. Windows turn into eyes and doors look like mouths. On the left is a particularly horrible row. The shapes are fairly simple, so you could try drawing your own.

Shadow spider plant

Shadows can easily become monsters. See how the plant below casts a horrible spidery shadow on the wall behind.

Try it yourself. Put a plant on a table by a wall in a dark room. Shine a flashlight or lamp on it to make a shadow on the wall. Different plants will make different shapes.

To draw it, first do the plant and pot and color them in. Put a patch of yellow behind and then smudge charcoal around the edges. Finally add the big black shadow.

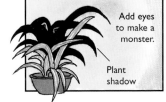

Add eyes to make a monster.

Plant shadow

Convertible car

Here are four steps to help you convert an ordinary car

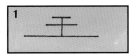

Draw one line down with three lines across it (at the top, bottom and a third of the way down). Each line across is twice as long as the line above and is cut in half by the down line.

For a bumper do three lines right across below the lights. The wheels are squares below the bumper. Do lines for the grille between the lights.

into a monstrous, menacing-looking beast.

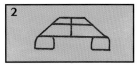

Join the ends of the lines. Do two squares for the headlights below the bottom line.

4 Adapt the shape to make your car look alive. Use curved lines. Make the lights into eyes with slit pupils. Turn the grille into fangs.

Dragons

Dragons are legendary monsters that lurk in dungeons and caves. They can be friendly but many are dangerous. Here are some dragons to draw.

Fairytale dragon

Most dragons have scaly skin, wings and evil teeth and claws. Follow boxes 1 to 4 to draw a classic fairytale dragon. You can see how to color it at the bottom of the page.*

1 Head and neck	2 Body and legs	3 Wing

Copy the picture on the left to draw the head, neck and bulging eye. Add nostrils, the other eye and spines down the neck as shown.	Draw lines for the top and bottom of the body. Add the legs. Erase the parts shown dotted above.	Draw a fan-shaped wing, as above. It looks like part of an umbrella, with spokes going from the bottom up to the point at the top.

Eye sockets

Nostrils

Put darker fingerprints on top of the body color, for scales.

See how to color the tail to show how it coils.

Add fiery breath.

Claws

4 Tail

A

B

Add the tail to the back of the body. Join line A to the top of the body and line B (shown in red on the left) to the underneath. Erase the dotted part.

Painting ideas

Body: green
Scales: when the body is dry, add dark green fingerprints.
Teeth and claws: yellow

Wings: pale yellow-green. Do the outline and spokes in dark green.
Mouth and eye: red
Nostril: black.

*Or use one of the ideas for coloring dinosaurs on pages 52-53.

A dragon's lair

To make a dragon that glows in a dark lair like this one, use chalk pastels on black paper.

First, draw the dragon's body. Add wings, claws, eyes and so on in bright colors.

For the fiery breath, draw wavy chalk lines and smudge them with a finger.

Do rocky walls in yellow. Smudge red and yellow on them to show how they are lit by the flames. Make heaps of dragon treasure with splotches of orange, red, green and blue.

Glowing dragon

Here is a way to make dragons that seem to glow in the dark. You need wax crayons, white paper and something pointed, like a knitting needle. *Always be very careful with pointed things.*

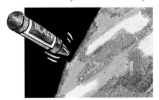

1. Start by coloring patches of bright wax crayon. Cover them with a thick layer of black crayon, as above.

2. Scratch a dragon's head into the black wax with a knitting needle. Bright colors will glow through.

3. Your monster will shine out of the blackness, like this.

*Go to **www.usborne-quicklinks.com** for a link to a Web site where you can find lots of pictures of dragons to print out and interactive games to play.*

63

Giants, ogres and trolls

There are giants in stories from around the world. They are scary because they are so huge. Try some of the tricks shown here to help you draw them.

How to draw a giant

A whole giant is about seven times the length of his head. The circles next to this giant are the size of his head, so you can see how many head-lengths different parts of his body are.

Arms reach about halfway down the thighs

1 head

Neck-waist 2 heads

Waist-knee 2 heads

Knee-foot 2 heads

You can draw people in the same way. They are seven times their head-length, too. Children only measure about five of their head-lengths, though.

How to make him look big

To show how big a giant is, put things in a picture to compare him with. In the picture below, see how the giant compares with the man, his dog and the trees.

The giant has to bend down to peer at the man and his dog.

A fairytale giant often wears clothes like tied leggings, a tunic and a big leather belt.

Spying giant

Try drawing a giant peering into a house through a window. You can tell how huge he is because his face takes up nearly the whole window frame.

When ogres look small

Castle is far away, so it is drawn small.

The ogre is nearly as tall as the tree next to him.

The boy only comes a little way up the tree next to him.

The bird is drawn big as it is closest to you.

In this picture, the boy is drawn as big as the ogre because he is closer to you. Things that are close to you look bigger than things far away.

In the same way, the trees closer to you are drawn bigger than the ones in the distance.

Compare each figure to the tree next to it to judge its true size.

The way things seem to get smaller in the distance is called perspective. You can use it to make pictures look realistic.

Looking up at a troll

If you were standing at the feet of an enormous troll, looking up, he would look a little like this.

Ask a grown-up if you can lie on the floor and look up at them to see for yourself. Their feet look huge, while the rest of their body and head seem small.

The way the parts furthest from you look squashed up and the closest parts seem to spread out wide is called foreshortening.

See the hints around the picture for how to draw a troll from down below.

Make the legs and body smaller as they go up.

Do a small head with squashed-up features.

His hands look big because they are closer to you.

Draw enormous feet closest to you.

65

Goblins, dwarfs and human horrors

All the creatures on these two pages have a head, two arms and two legs, like ordinary people. But these are supernatural beings that live underground, fly at night or haunt dark dungeons.

Skeleton

This is a spooky human skeleton. It has been drawn simpler than a real skeleton, which has hundreds of bones and is very hard to draw. Follow the instructions around the picture to help you draw one yourself.

For a skull, first draw the dome of the head and eye sockets.

Add the teeth and the jaw.

Color the eye sockets black and add a hole for the nose.

The spine has lots of small bones. Draw them close but not touching.

Ribs curve and get shorter near the waist.

This is the pelvis bone. It joins the spine and legs.

Legs and arms have two long, narrow bones each. See how they join at the elbows and knees.

Use pale gray and yellow to color the skeleton.

Feet and hands have lots of small bones.

Dwarfs

Dwarfs have short bodies and legs, but big heads, hands and feet. They are usually tubby, with bushy beards.

The dwarfs in this picture are in their forge. They are quite tricky to draw. You could trace them, then try to color them yourself.

Faces and fronts lit by flames

Colors get darker away from fire.

Hammer

Bellows

Tongs

Anvil

66

Witch's silhouette

To get the witch's shape, follow these steps:

1. Draw these shapes:

Head
Body
Broomstick
Skirt

2. Add details and erase extra lines.

Hat
Face
Cloak
Arm
Feet
Twigs

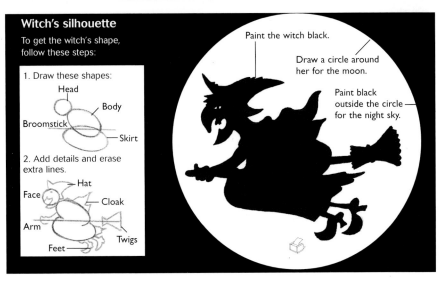

Paint the witch black.

Draw a circle around her for the moon.

Paint black outside the circle for the night sky.

Tunnel disappears into darkness here

Draw shoulders jutting from the side of its head, so it looks as though its head is sunk low.

Do arms reaching below the knees.

Drawing goblins

To draw a goblin, do a thin human shape. Give it knobbly knees and elbows and long, skinny arms, Give it a narrow head with pointed ears, and color it green with glowing eyes.

Try drawing this advancing horde of goblins in a tunnel. Put big goblins at the front of your picture and smaller ones behind. Make the tunnel floor get narrower in the distance, and the walls get closer in. This is using perspective (see page 65 for more about this).

67

Techniques and materials

Here is a summary of all the techniques and materials used in this part of the book. The chart on the right has a column for each material, telling you how you can use it. A white panel across more than one column refers to all the materials in those columns.

Red

Red and yellow make orange.

Mix red, yellow and blue to make brown.

Yellow

Blue

Blue and red make purple.

Yellow and blue make green.

Mixing colors

This color monster shows you which colors mix to make other colors. You only need red, yellow and blue to make all these colors. (Felt-tip pens do not mix like this.) Use black to make them darker, and white to make them paler.

The pencil family

Pencils can be hard or soft. Soft pencils make thick, fuzzy lines. Hard pencils make thin, clear lines. Most pencils are marked with a code to tell you how hard or soft they are. See how the code works on the right.

2H   H   HB   B   2B

Harder: up to 12H | Softer: up to 12B

Most ordinary writing pencils are HB.

Using fixative sprays

Fixative sprays stop pictures in soft materials like charcoal, chalk and soft pencil from smudging. They come in spray cans and you can get them from art suppliers.

Never breathe the spray or work near a flame. It is best to use them outside, since they smell very strong. Never throw empty cans on a fire.

Colored pencils	Pencils
Colored pencils are good for hairy effects.	You probably use pencils the most. You can draw with them first even if you color afterward.

Drawing lines

Use the point of pencils or colored pencils for fine lines and the side of the point for fuzzy lines and shading.

Shading with lines and dots

You can create shadows using lines or dots – the closer you draw them, the deeper the shadow.

Make different shades with colored pencil by pressing lighter or harder.

Textures

Make different skin textures by rubbing over things placed under your paper (see page 53).

Charcoal	Chalk pastels	Wax crayons	Paint	Ink	Felt-tip pens

Shading

Lie a stick of charcoal, chalk or a wax crayon on its side and rub. You can snap the sticks to make them smaller if necessary.

Chalk pastels show up well on black paper.

Use chalk to make double prints (page 56).

Using the side of the point

Scrape shapes into layers of wax crayon (see page 63) or into paint on top of wax.

Spots and splashes

Paint and ink are liquid (paint may be powdery or hard, but you add water to it). Drop blobs of paint from a brush (see page 59), or shake ink blots from a pen nib. Spray paint or ink from an old toothbrush (pages 57 and 70).

Thick felt-tips are good for making solid areas of color. Thin ones are good for lines and details.

Hatching

Draw parallel lines like this across the part you want to shade.

Cross-hatching

Draw two sets of lines criss-crossing for darker shadows.

Stippling

Shade with dots. More dots, closer together, make darker areas.

Smudging

Smudge soft pencils, chalk and charcoal with your finger. See the fuzzy alien on page 57 for an example.

Use wax crayons and chalk pastels to make double prints, as on page 56.

Wax and water don't mix. You can use this to make good contrasts (see page 59).

Washes

Make a wash background with streaks of paint or ink on paper soaked with water. See how on page 59.

Using an eraser

Use an eraser to make marks in pencils, charcoal and chalk. See an example on page 55.

Prints

Dip your fingers in paint or ink and make prints. See how to use them on page 62. You can make prints with other things, such as those below.

Felt-tip pens come in lots of colors, including luminous ones, but they do not mix well. You can use dark ones on top of light ones, though.

Try using coins, feathers or wood. Textures show best with crayons, pencils, charcoal or chalk.

Thread spool

Matchbox

Polystyrene chip

People or monsters?

The monsters on this page are people of a kind – or at least, they might be.

The Yeti seems to blend into the snow.

Yeti

Yetis are said to live in the Himalayas. No one knows if they are a type of person, ape or monster. Draw this one on blue paper or paint a blue background.

Paint a shaggy Yeti with white paint on a brush. Use as little water as possible so the paint is fairly dry and goes on in rough streaks. Add a blizzard whirling around him.

Werewolf

This ordinary-looking man turns into a terrifying werewolf on nights when there is a full moon. Try drawing him in stages as he changes.

You can color him with colored pencils. Use light layers of brown, yellow and pink for his skin, and shades of brown for his hair.

As he changes, his face is pulled forward: make his nose longer and his chin stick out. Give him a longer, thinner mouth, draw his ear higher up and pointed and make him sprout hair on his chin, cheeks and forehead.

Fully changed, he looks like a fierce wolf. Draw a wolf's muzzle. Add sharp teeth and glowing red eyes. His ears are now almost on top of his head. He is hairy all over.

You can make a blizzard by spraying white paint from a toothbrush, as on page 57.

Go to **www.usborne-quicklinks.com** for a link to a Web site where you can find out about other monster legends around the world. See if you can draw some of them.

Internet links

For more information about drawing monsters, go to the Usborne Quicklinks Web site at **www.usborne-quicklinks.com** and click on the number of the Web site you want to visit.

Web site 1 This Web site has an excellent step-by-step guide to drawing dinosaurs from a professional dinosaur artist.

Web site 2 Phantom hounds, werewolves, vampires and other scary creatures – you'll find out all about them, and see some artists' impressions and even photographs on this site.

Web site 3 Choose from different alien heads, bodies and legs to fit together, or try drawing aliens in 3-D or even making them out of papier mâché.

Web site 4 Download some clip art aliens. There are several pages to choose from. You could use them to make cards or posters on your computer, or you could try copying them for drawing practice.

Web site 5 Friendly cartoon monsters can be easy to draw. Take a look at this gallery of monsters for some ideas. You can also send monster e-greetings and watch some monster animations.

Web site 6 At this site, you can read some of the weird and wonderful stories and theories about UFOs and aliens.

Web site 7 The deep ocean is home to some amazing real-life monsters. Try drawing some of them.

Web site 8 Read the theories and see artists' impressions of Nessie, the most famous underwater monster of them all.

Web site 9 You'll find lots of ideas for monster drawings in the Greek myths, such as the three-headed hound Cerberus. At this site, you can read some light-hearted retellings of the classic stories.

Web site 10 Follow a series of easy steps to create a different creature every week and find some handy drawing tips.

Web site 11 The strangest creatures can appear in your dreams. Read about some famous artists and their dream creations, or try drawing from your own dreams.

Web site 12 Here, you can watch a trailer and meet the characters of the Disney movie "Monsters, Inc." There are free movie screensavers and desktop wallpapers to download, too.

HOW TO DRAW
MACHINES

Moira Butterfield and Anita Ganeri

Designed by Kim Blundell and Robert Walster

Illustrated by Kim Blundell, Chris Lyon, Steve Cross,
Peter Bull and Graham Round

Additional designs by Steve Page

CONTENTS

74 Drawing machines
76 Cars
80 Big vehicles
81 Ships and boats
82 Trains
84 Planes

86 Bicycles and motorcycles
88 Robots
90 Space machines
92 Batty inventions
94 Drawing from life
95 Internet links

Drawing machines

If you are interested in machines, you may also enjoy drawing them. This section shows you techniques for drawing all kinds of machines, from vintage cars to spacecraft.

You can find out how to draw realistic pictures of machines you see around you, such as cars, trains, planes and cycles.

There are also tips on drawing cartoon machines – making them look funny and friendly, or fierce and frightening.

You can use your imagination to invent fantasy machines, such as robots and spaceships. There are lots of ideas to start you off.

At the end of this section, there are some professional tips on how to make drawings of machines from real life.

Drawing tips

Before you start drawing, here is some basic information about different drawing materials and how to use them to create different effects in your pictures.

For rough sketches and experiments, you can draw on pieces of scrap paper. For more finished drawings you may prefer to use Bristol or copier paper, which is better quality but is not too expensive.

Materials and shading

Paints, inks and thick felt-tip pens give flat areas of color. These are good for simple pictures and diagrams. Use darker shades of the main color to do the shading.

This shape is on page 76.

Copying pictures

You can use this method to copy a picture. It will help you to figure out how the picture was drawn.

Use a ruler to measure out a grid.

You could use this method to copy the pictures in this book.

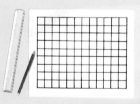

1. On tracing paper, draw a grid made up of equal-sized squares, like the one above. Make the grid large enough to cover the whole picture.

---

*Go to **www.usborne-quicklinks.com** for a link to a Web site where you can find out how to practice drawing basic shapes using thumbnail sketches.*

Pencils, colored pencils and fine felt-tip pens give a clear outline. You can use them for hatching (a way of shading using straight lines).

Use straight lines to shade flat surfaces and curved lines for rounded surfaces.

Crossed lines, called cross-hatching, are used for darker shading. This technique works well on flat surfaces.

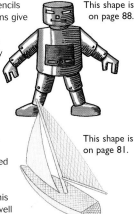

This shape is on page 88.

This shape is on page 81.

Charcoal and chalk can be used for big pictures. You can shade by smudging the lines with your finger. You can also smudge soft lead pencil in the same way.

This shape is on page 82.

For shading in felt-tips, colored pencil or paint, you can use streaks of color. Use several different shades of the same color to fill in an area, leaving some white streaks for highlights.

This shape is on page 87.

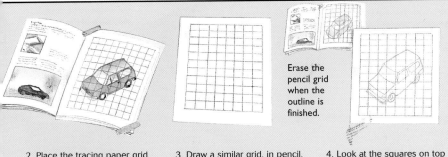

Erase the pencil grid when the outline is finished.

2. Place the tracing paper grid over the picture you want to copy. Tape or weigh the paper down to stop it from slipping.

3. Draw a similar grid, in pencil, on a sheet of paper. Use the same number of squares, as big or as small as you like.

4. Look at the squares on top of the picture. Copy the shapes in each one into the same square on the drawing paper.

Go to www.usborne-quicklinks.com for a link to a Web site where you can learn about color and shading and find some tips for practicing your shading techniques.

75

Cars

Cars are made up of simple shapes and are fairly easy to draw. You can make them look sleek and shiny, or you can draw cartoon cars with human faces.

There are suggestions for a wide range of car pictures on the next four pages. Looking at a real car, or a photo of one, will help you to get the shapes right.

A car shape

The lines shown in green should be upright and parallel.

The lines shown in pink should be parallel.*

To draw an angled view of a car, sketch two slanting boxes in pencil, like the ones above. You can erase them later.

Draw a car shape inside the boxes.

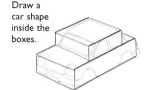

Add sides to the box to give a more solid shape. Use the boxes to help you figure out the outline of your car.

All the lines in the same color should be parallel.

If you want to vary the angle of the car, change the angle of the two boxes you draw to start with.

Coloring in

Once you have drawn the car shape, you can color it in and finish it off as shown here.

Add side mirrors.

Make bumper shiny.

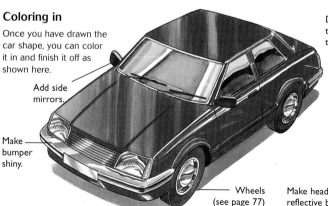

Draw shadowy shapes in the windows to suggest the inside of the car.

To make the paintwork shiny, use streaks of light and dark color. White streaks give a polished look.

Wheels (see page 77)

Make headlights look reflective by using multi-colored flashes.

*These lines would in fact be slightly closer together at the back of the car, due to perspective, but for this simple drawing you can draw them parallel. See page 83 for more about perspective.

Drawing a wheel

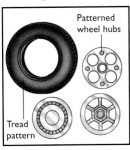

You can make a car tire look rounded by using gray shading, as above. Add a light gray tread pattern and a wheel hub.

Patterned wheel hubs

Tread pattern

Draw a curve to show the inside edge of the wheel hub.

To show a wheel at an angle, draw an oval shape on the side of the car body, and draw in a smaller oval for the wheel hub.

Erase the line here.

Shade in the gap behind the wheel.

Front edge

Erase the part of the oval that goes over the car body. Draw in the front edge of the wheel, and shade it in.

Custom cars

Some people "customize" cars as a hobby. That means they add their own special decorations to make totally original-looking vehicles. On the right are some suggestions for you to copy or trace.

Blobmobile

Flaming speedster

Zebra Mark I

Flower power

Sports car

Sports cars have a streamlined shape, to help them go faster. You can get this effect by starting with the shape on the right.

Sports cars often have special features like the ones in this picture.

Wedge-shaped front | Sloping back

This car has been done in three shades of the same color. The background and road are blurred to show speed.

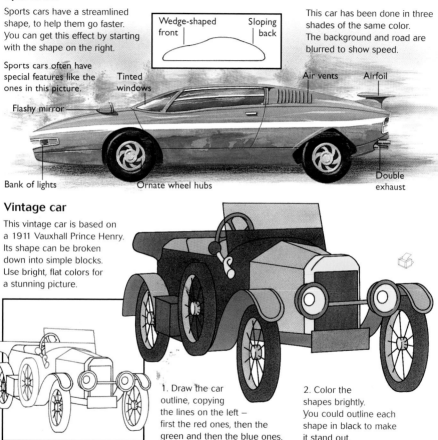

Flashy mirror

Tinted windows

Air vents

Airfoil

Bank of lights

Ornate wheel hubs

Double exhaust

Vintage car

This vintage car is based on a 1911 Vauxhall Prince Henry. Its shape can be broken down into simple blocks. Use bright, flat colors for a stunning picture.

1. Draw the car outline, copying the lines on the left — first the red ones, then the green and then the blue ones.

2. Color the shapes brightly. You could outline each shape in black to make it stand out.

Go to **www.usborne-quicklinks.com** for a link to a Web site where you'll find photos of all kinds of cars, from vintage cars to modern ones. Use them for ideas.

Cartoon cars

You can give cars different characters when you draw them as cartoons. Use car parts, such as the headlights or the grille, to give the car human features such as eyes, mouths and eyebrows. Here are some examples of how to do this.

Draw a friendly car with a round, bright body and wheels bending inward. You could use the grille as a smiling mouth, the hood ornament as a nose and the headlights as eyes.

This fierce car has a square, sharp-cornered body and big wheels. Add narrow, shifty eyes and use the front wings as eyebrows. Draw a row of sharp teeth in the grille.

Draw a worn-out car with a dented body, flat tires, a cracked window and battered paintwork. Make the grille into a sad mouth and turn the headlights into droopy eyes.

Fast and slow

You can show how a car is moving by changing its shape. For example, this car looks as though it is speeding around a bend in the road. Curve all of the body lines around the bend, and add curved speed lines to show that the car is moving really fast.

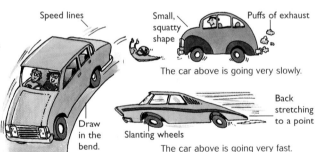

Speed lines

Draw in the bend.

Small, squatty shape

Puffs of exhaust

The car above is going very slowly.

Back stretching to a point

Slanting wheels

The car above is going very fast.

Crazy cars

You can make all kinds of unlikely objects into crazy cartoon cars. Here are some ideas.

Big vehicles

On this page you can find out how to draw bigger, chunkier-looking vehicles such as trucks, tractors and tankers. These are fun to draw because they are made up of big, solid shapes, and you can use bold, bright colors.

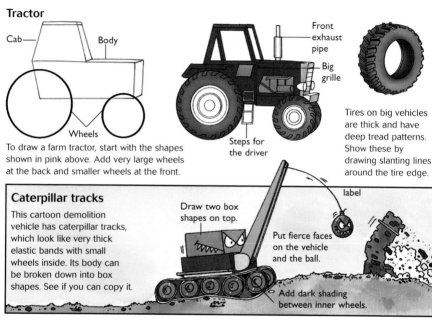

Tractor

Cab

Body

Wheels

To draw a farm tractor, start with the shapes shown in pink above. Add very large wheels at the back and smaller wheels at the front.

Front exhaust pipe

Big grille

Steps for the driver

Tires on big vehicles are thick and have deep tread patterns. Show these by drawing slanting lines around the tire edge.

Caterpillar tracks

This cartoon demolition vehicle has caterpillar tracks, which look like very thick elastic bands with small wheels inside. Its body can be broken down into box shapes. See if you can copy it.

Draw two box shapes on top.

label

Put fierce faces on the vehicle and the ball.

Add dark shading between inner wheels.

Convoy

You could make a wall frieze based on the trucks on the right. Copy them freehand, or use a grid (see pages 74-75). Add cars (pages 76-79), motorcycles and bicycles (pages 86-87) if you like.

Shading to show shine on windows

Delivery truck

Shading to show ridges

Dump truck

Shading to show cylinder shape

Tanker

Ships and boats

Here you can see how to draw ships and boats, building them up from simple shapes. There are also some coloring techniques for you to experiment.

Ship shapes

The shape of an object appears to change, depending on where you are standing when you look at it. This position is called your viewpoint.

The horizon is generally level with your viewpoint. Here you can see how some ships look from different angles.

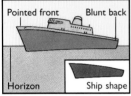

To show that you are level with the ship, put the horizon line half way up the picture.

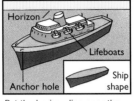

Put the horizon line near the top to show that you are looking down on the ship.

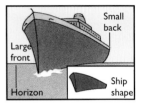

To show that you are looking up at the ship, make the horizon line low.

Racing yacht

This racing yacht is done in a sketchy style. Use sharp colored pencils to scribble on the colors.

1. Draw the yacht outline in faint pencil to start with, copying the shape shown in the box on the right.

2. Scribble in the mast and sail. Scribble stripes on the sails and some people shapes on the deck.

3. Go over the hull shape with colored pencil, leaving out the lines behind the sails. Use green and white pencils to scribble in sea.

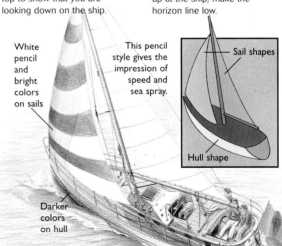

White pencil and bright colors on sails

This pencil style gives the impression of speed and sea spray.

Darker colors on hull

Trains

Trains make striking pictures because of their chunky shapes. Here you can see how to draw old-fashioned steam trains and modern high-speed models.

Steam trains

To make a steam train shape, begin by drawing a cylinder in pencil. Start with an oval and then add two lines and a curve, as shown on the right. Add some wheels at an angle, and join them together with rods. You can then add other extras such as a funnel, buffers, tracks and a driver's cab. Use felt-tip pens for bright, flat colors.

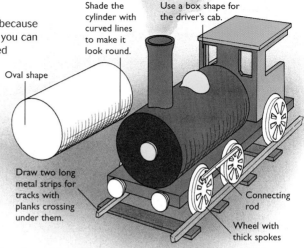

Shade the cylinder with curved lines to make it look round.

Use a box shape for the driver's cab.

Oval shape

Draw two long metal strips for tracks with planks crossing under them.

Connecting rod

Wheel with thick spokes

Train shape

Use your finger to smudge the charcoal in a curve around the cylinder shape.

Smoke and soot

This steam train is drawn in charcoal and chalk for a sooty, smoky look. You can get this effect by following the steps below.

1. Start your picture by sketching the basic train shape with a thin charcoal line. You can copy the shape from the box on the left.

2. Using the charcoal, color the body a light gray and make the shadowy parts darker. Use white chalk to highlight the shiniest parts.

3. Color in the smoke with chalk and charcoal. Use your finger to smudge them together in circles to get a dramatic billowing effect.*

High-speed models

Modern trains are long and streamlined and sometimes have pointed fronts. You don't need to draw wheels on them. A dark shadow under the body gives a good impression of speed.

Blurred background

Horizontal lines show speed

Parts of an object look smaller the further away they are. This is called perspective. A train speeding forward looks big at the front and narrows to a point, called the vanishing point, at the back.

The vanishing point, where the top and bottom of the train seem to meet

Make wheels, windows and doors smaller the further away they are.

Trains with brains

You can draw train cartoons by exaggerating the way the trains move, and by giving them human faces. Here are some suggestions.

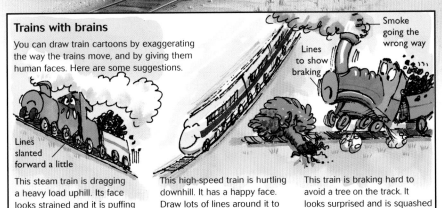

Smoke going the wrong way

Lines to show braking

Lines slanted forward a little

This steam train is dragging a heavy load uphill. Its face looks strained and it is puffing out lots of steam.

This high-speed train is hurtling downhill. It has a happy face. Draw lots of lines around it to give the idea of speed.

This train is braking hard to avoid a tree on the track. It looks surprised and is squashed up and leaning backward.

Go to **www.usborne-quicklinks.com** for a link to a Web site where you can try drawing one of the earliest high-speed trains and find out about its streamlined design.

Planes

Planes can make spectacular pictures because of their sleek, streamlined shapes. You need to make the surface look shiny on the smooth wings and body.

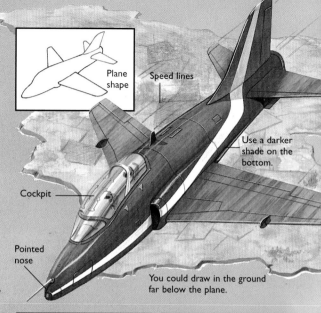

Plane shape

Speed lines

Use a darker shade on the bottom.

Cockpit

Pointed nose

You could draw in the ground far below the plane.

Jet plane

To draw a jet plane, like the Hawk shown here, start with the long, thin shape, shown in red on the box above. Then add wings, shown in blue, and a tailplane, shown in green.

Paint or color the body to give a smooth surface, and add pale highlights to make it look shiny.

Take-off

Follow these three steps to draw a plane taking off above you.

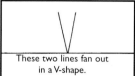

These two lines fan out in a V-shape.

Add shapes of buildings along the horizon.

Draw a horizon line across the paper. In faint pencil, draw two straight lines fanning out from the center of the horizon line. Use a ruler to help you get an accurate shape.

Draw the plane as shown above, using the lines fanning outward as the sides of the plane body. Color it in, adding silhouettes of the airport on the horizon.

Draw lines fanning out toward you for the runway. Add white star shapes along each of the lines to show the runway lights. Make the stars bigger toward the front.

Go to www.usborne-quicklinks.com for a link to a Web site where you'll find hundreds of photos of planes to draw.

Formation flying

To draw a formation flying team, repeat the plane shape shown in the box on the right several times, in any flying pattern you like. You could draw your picture on a bright blue background with trails of different colored smoke behind the planes.

Draw smoke trails with a series of curves, like this.

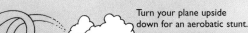

Use one bright team color for the plane shapes.

Plane shape

Sky writer

This cartoon sky-writing plane has a round body and a fat tail and wings. Add a cheerful face and a black nose. Make its smoke trail spell a word or show a pattern of curls and twists.

Bi-plane

Start this picture of a bi-plane by drawing a triangular nose. Then add the wings, with struts and pieces of wire criss-crossed between them. Add the wheels, which are joined together by another strut. Add two tailpieces sticking out from behind the nose, and a pilot sitting on top. Draw two lines forming loops to show the path made by the plane's exhaust trail.

Turn your plane upside down for an aerobatic stunt.

Draw a bird to show the plane is upside down. 85

Bicycles and motorcycles

Bicycle shapes are fairly complicated, so it is a good idea to do a pencil sketch of your drawing first. Once you have got the shape right you can color it in.

On these pages you can see how to draw action-packed pictures of bicycles and motorcycles, and how to give them a professional finish.

Drawing a bicycle

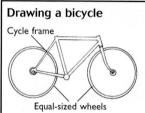

Cycle frame

Equal-sized wheels

Start by drawing two round wheels of equal size. The space between them should be about half the width of one wheel. Put a wheel hub in the center of each, and draw the cycle frame.

Saddle   Handlebars

Chain

Pedal   Chain wheel

Draw the chain wheel, the chain and the other parts shown above. Color the cycle frame brightly, and add pale streaks to make it shiny. Color the metal parts streaky gray.

Go over the pencil outline with black pen.

Wheel spokes

Draw a few wheel spokes. Make some pale and some dark, to suggest light reflecting off them. Color the wheels black, with a metallic-looking band around the inside.

People on cycles

Here are some pictures of people riding cycles. The stick figures drawn in red are to help you draw the people in the right position.

Do the stick figures in light pencil, then gradually build up the body shapes around them. You can erase the pencil when you have finished.

Side view

Draw lines to show the wheel moving.

Front view

Stunt cycle

Motorcycles

To do a picture of a shiny, streamlined motorcycle, follow the steps here.

Cycle shape

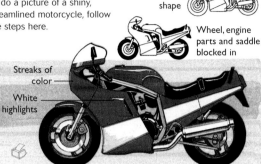

Wheel, engine parts and saddle blocked in

Streaks of color

White highlights

1. Use the grid method on pages 74-75 to copy the main shapes of the motorcycle from the finished picture above. Block in the dark areas with one color.

2. Make the paintwork look shiny by shading it in streaks, using felt-tip pens in different shades of the same color. Leave the shiniest part of the body white, or add white highlights.

Super-shine

For a super-shiny look, try drawing a motorcycle outline in white colored pencil or chalk*

on black paper. Shade in the shiniest parts and leave the rest of the cycle black.

You will need to fix a chalk picture afterward (see page 94).

Fun cycles

Lines to show shaking

This cartoon cycle is being ridden over rough ground. It is drawn with a wiggly, shaky outline.

Start this dragster with a triangle shape. The rider has to lean back a long way in the seat.

Speed lines

The basic shape of a rider seen from behind is similar to the front view shown on page 86.

Robots

You can have lots of fun drawing robots because they can be any shape, size or color you like. Below are some ideas for robot pictures to start you off.

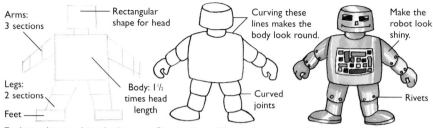

Arms: 3 sections

Rectangular shape for head

Legs: 2 sections

Feet

Body: 1½ times head length

Curving these lines makes the body look round.

Curved joints

Make the robot look shiny.

Rivets

To draw a human-shaped robot, first do a pencil sketch, using simple block shapes to get the size right.

Go over the outline in ink or felt-tip pen, making the body shape rounder. Erase pencil marks and color the robot.

Give the robot a face, and put a control panel covered in knobs on its chest. Add some dots for rivets.

Robot assortment

You can use all kinds of shapes to draw robots. Below is an assortment of heads, bodies and legs. You could copy or trace these parts,

and mix and match them to make up your own robot. Use bright colors and add any other extras you like.

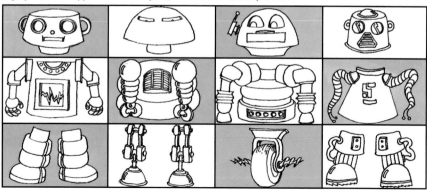

Special robots

Drawing this robot from below makes it look bigger and fiercer. The body gets narrower as it gets further away.

You could try designing a robot to do a special job. This robot has nine arms so it can do lots of household chores at once.

This robot has gone wrong. Its arms and legs are out of control, and there are electric sparks coming out of its control panel.

Crazy eyes

Zigzags and stars to show electric sparks

Robots you know

Here you can see how to make some of the people and animals you know look like robots. Give them robot bodies but add features so they can be recognized.

Granny robot

Teacher robot

Cat robot

Dog robot

Robot T-shirt

Robot control

Press here

Decorate a white T-shirt with a robot control panel. You will need to use special pens for coloring on fabric. You can buy these in craft stores.

Go to **www.usborne-quicklinks.com** for a link to a Web site where you can see some "robot pets". Try drawing one and some of its tricks.

Space machines

On these two pages there are lots of space machine drawings for you to try, using paints, colored pencils or crayons.

Shuttle launch

To draw this dramatic space shuttle launch, follow the steps below.

1. Draw the shuttle in three stages, copying the outline on the right. Do the plane-shaped part first, then the fuel tank, then the two rocket boosters.

2. Color the shuttle using paints or colored pencils. Streak the colors or add white highlights to make it look shiny.

3. Color in a cloud of exhaust all around the shuttle, using white, yellow, orange, red and gray.

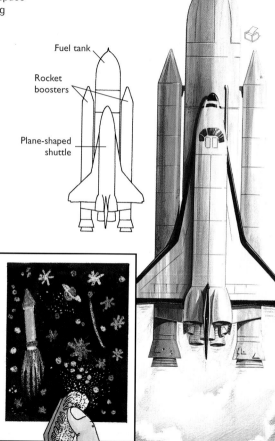

Fuel tank

Rocket boosters

Plane-shaped shuttle

Out in space

You could try drawing rockets and planets on white paper, using brightly-colored wax crayons. Then cover the whole picture with a wash of black paint.* The crayon will show through the wash.

When it is dry, you can add some bright stars. Dip an old toothbrush in white paint. Hold it bristles-down over the paper and run your finger toward you along the bristles.

*Tape the picture down on a flat surface while the paint dries, to stop it from crinkling.

On the Moon

Here you can see how to draw a picture of the Apollo 11 Lunar Module, the first spacecraft to put a man on the Moon.

1. Use the grid method shown on pages 74-75 to copy the outline in red below.

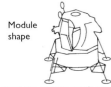

Module shape

This lunar module landed on the Moon on 20 July 1969.

2. Paint the bottom section to look like reflective gold foil, by splotching on yellow, orange and white watercolor paint, so that the colors run together.

3. Paint the top section gray, with shiny-looking white parts and dark, shadowy lines to suggest equipment shapes. Paint in the legs and the ladder.

4. Paint the moonscape in shades of gray, with crater shapes. You could add some footprints coming from the craft. Paint the sky black, with stars.

Space station

To draw this space station, start with the outline below.

Color in the space station. Add the parts labeled on the right.

To draw the spacewalking astronaut, start with lots of circle shapes, as shown on the right. Then draw a body outline around the circles.

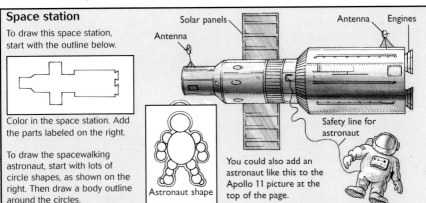

Solar panels

Antenna

Antenna   Engines

Safety line for astronaut

Astronaut shape

You could also add an astronaut like this to the Apollo 11 picture at the top of the page.

Go to www.usborne-quicklinks.com for a link to a Web site with a vast space picture archive. You can use the pictures to give you ideas, or to help you draw details accurately.

91

Batty inventions

Before you draw your own batty invention, first decide what you want it to do. On these pages are some ideas to start you off, showing you how to make your machine work using parts such as cogs, wheels and rivets.

Heath Robinson

W. Heath Robinson was a famous British illustrator of the 1930s. He was especially well known for his pictures of amazing inventions. He made them up using lots of objects joined together in unexpected ways. Each invention was designed to do a special job. The picture on the right is a Heath Robinson idea for a potato peeling machine.*

Trying it yourself

You could try drawing your own invention using everyday bits and pieces joined together in original ways. Draw in arrows and labels to show how the parts fit together.

Blueprints

Blueprints are photographic copies of designs. These may be given to the manufacturers of a machine, to show how all its parts fit together.

To make a drawing look like a blueprint, do it as an outline in dark blue colored pencil on pale blue paper, like the two contraptions on the right.

Tea pourer

Cleaning machine

*Reproduced by kind permission of Laurence Pollinger Ltd. and the estate of Mrs. J. C. Robinson.

Plant waterer

The plant waterer on the right uses rope, a see-saw, springs, cogs and balls to make the watering can tip over and water the flowers. Can you see how?

You could try adapting this drawing to make it into a shower spray attached to the bathtub. Think how the different parts go together to make the machine work as a whole.

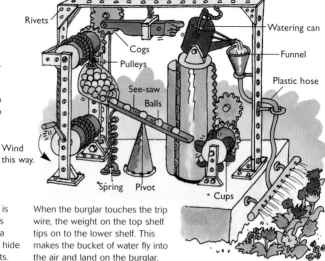

Rivets

Cogs

Pulleys

See-saw

Balls

Wind this way.

Spring

Pivot

Watering can

Funnel

Plastic hose

Cups

Burglar trap

This idea for a burglar trap is fairly simple to draw. It uses wire, weights, shelves and a bucket of water. You could hide the wire among some plants.

When the burglar touches the trip wire, the weight on the top shelf tips on to the lower shelf. This makes the bucket of water fly into the air and land on the burglar.

Weight

Rod

Pivot

Shelf

Bucket

Trip wire

IDEAS LIST

Here are some other suggestions for you to try drawing:

Morning alarm

Seed planter

Shower spray

Pet feeder

Drawing from life

To do an accurate drawing of a machine that is in front of you, look at it carefully. Note how wide it is compared with how high it is, and how different parts compare with each other in size. Check the proportions using your thumb and a pencil as shown below.

1. With one eye closed, hold a pencil out at arm's length. Line up the pencil with one of the edges on the object.

2. Mark the length of the edge by positioning the pencil end at the top and your thumb on the pencil level with the bottom edge.

3. Keeping your thumb in the same position, check how many times this length fits into other parts of the object.

4. Check that the proportions in your drawing compare with each other in a similar way. If they do not, alter your sketch.

Shadows

To get the shadows in the right place on a realistic picture, first see which direction the light is coming from. Then put shadows on areas that are hidden from the light.

Don't forget to show background shadows around any objects you draw. This makes a picture look more realistic.*

These parts are hidden from the light.

Avoiding smudges

Charcoal, chalk and soft pencil smudge easily. You can stop this by spraying a fixative over your finished picture. You can buy fixative from art supply stores. Always use it in a well-ventilated area, and never spray near a flame.

*Different kinds of shading are shown on page 75.

Internet links

For more information about drawing machines, go to the Usborne Quicklinks Web site at **www.usborne-quicklinks.com** and click on the number of the Web site you want to visit.

Web site 1 If you're interested in drawing racing cars, this site has lots of action pictures to give you ideas.

Web site 2 Try drawing some of the photos of US Navy ships, submarines and aircraft at work from this Web site.

Web site 3 Historic trains can be fairly complicated to draw, so try using some of these pictures as a guide. Click on **Collections** and then **Focus on locomotives**.

Web site 4 Here, you'll find photos and paintings of historic planes, with stories about them and the people who flew them.

Web site 5 This site has lots of photos of bicycles from 1816 to the present day.

Web site 6 Here you'll find hundreds of photos of space and spacecraft. You might like to put some of them in your space pictures or print them out to use in projects.

Web site 7 You could try designing your own robot on this fun, interactive Web site.

Web site 8 This is a fascinating Web site about robots and robotics. You can find out how they are made and how they work, and there are even some robots created by artists.

Web site 9 Find out about Leonardo da Vinci, one of the greatest scientists, artists and inventors in history, at this site.

Web site 10 This site is full of space activities, pictures and information. You can print out templates to make model space shuttles, satellites and other space machines.

Web site 11 At this site, you can learn how to draw a sailing boat by following a step-by-step guide.

Web site 12 Have you ever wondered how planes actually fly, or how car engines work? At this Web site, you can watch short movies which explain how lots of different machines work. You'll need a set of speakers or headphones to listen to the movies.

Web site 13 This site has lots of tips for drawing space monsters and weird machines in 3-D.

Web site 14 At this site, you can explore an interactive timeline of inventions that have changed the way we live.

HOW TO DRAW
GHOSTS

Emma Fischel

Designed by Kim Blundell

Illustrated by Victor Ambrus, Kim Blundell, Rob McCaig,
Mike Pringle and Graham Round

Edited by Janet Cook and Anita Ganeri

CONTENTS

98 Drawing ghosts
100 Ghostly shapes
102 Some human ghosts
106 Ghosts from around
the world
108 Ghost train ride
110 Haunted houses
112 Inside the house
114 Mix and match
116 Vampires
118 Dracula
119 Internet links

Drawing ghosts

This part of the book shows you how to draw supernatural things. Some are funny – and some will send shivers down your spine.

Ghosts

On pages 100-109, you can find out how to draw all sorts of different ghosts. Use pages 100-101 to start you off. They show you how you can make simple shapes look ghostly by the way you paint them.

Pages 102-105 show you how to draw more ghostly effects, and on pages 106-109 you'll find spooky creatures from all around the world.

These watercolor ghosts are on page 100.

Vampires

Pages 116-118 show you how to draw vampires and all the horrible things associated with them. The picture of Dracula above is on page 118.

Cartoons

There are lots of ideas for funny cartoons in this section, like this person who has just seen a ghost.

Mixing pictures

You could combine different ideas in this section to make your own ghostly scene. Try drawing one of the vampires from page 116 lurking around the haunted house on pages 110-111, for example.

The inside of the house could also be a good setting for some of the ghosts on pages 100-105. On pages 114-115 there are lots of heads and bodies you could mix to create your own ghosts and vampires. You can put these in the haunted house or in other spooky settings.

Haunted houses

You can see how to draw a haunted house from the outside on pages 110-111. On pages 112-113 there are lots of ideas to help you draw what's inside the house, too.

*Go to **www.usborne-quicklinks.com** for a link to a Web site which has some tips on keeping sketchbooks.*

Drawing in stages

Many of the pictures in this book have step-by-step drawing instructions for you to follow. Always copy the outline shapes in pencil.

Draw the lines shown in green first, then those shown in red and lastly the ones shown in blue.

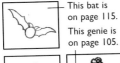

The easiest shapes to draw have just one outline.

This bat is on page 115.

This genie is on page 105.

More difficult shapes have two outlines.

Make the outlines the size you want your picture to be.

The hardest shapes to draw have three outlines.

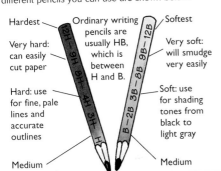

See page 108 for how to draw this ghoul.

Pencils

Pencils are marked with a code which tells you how hard or soft they are. Choose a pencil that suits the kind of drawing you want to do. The different pencils you can use are shown below.

Hardest

Very hard: can easily cut paper

Hard: use for fine, pale lines and accurate outlines

Medium

Ordinary writing pencils are usually HB, which is between H and B.

Softest

Very soft: will smudge very easily

Soft: use for shading tones from black to light gray

Medium

Using a fixative spray

Lots of the pictures in this section are drawn with charcoal, chalks or soft pencils. If you use these, you will need to use a fixative spray when you have finished the picture to stop it from smudging. You can buy the spray from art supply stores.

Hold your drawing upright and spray it from about 16in away. Use two light coats of spray; one heavy coat will discolor the paper.

This picture is on page 102.

Always use the spray in an open space, preferably outside, as the fumes are dangerous.

Go to **www.usborne-quicklinks.com** for a link to a Web site where you can find out what the story is behind an ordinary lead pencil.

Ghostly shapes

What are ghosts? Where do they come from and what do they look like? As no one really knows, there are no limits to the ways you can draw them. You need to capture the sense of mystery about them because, although people have been telling stories about them for hundreds of years, there is no proof that they even exist.

Here are a few ideas to start you on your way.

Ghostly background

A good background can help to create a ghostly atmosphere. Gloomy castle battlements drawn at an odd angle give this picture an uncomfortable feel.

Shadowy ghosts

These ghosts seem to be looming out of the darkness. To draw them, you will need to use a soft pencil* and a thin eraser. First shade all over a sheet of paper with the pencil, then erase some of the pencil shading to suggest the ghosts' outlines and faces.

Using watercolors

You can use watercolor paints to create the blurred and mysterious look of these ghosts. Follow the steps on the right to draw them.

Use a very faint pencil line to draw the ghosts' outline shapes. Make the shapes fairly big, so that you have a large enough surface on which to paint.

*See page 99 for the different kinds of pencils you can use.

Use pencil to draw first the ghost shape, then the outline of the castle.

Color the castle with thick felt-tip pens, using diagonal line strokes to fill in the pencil outline. Color the ghost with felt-tips and add drooping eyes and a mouth.

First paint the shapes with clean water, then paint streaks of watercolor on top. The colors will blend together, making new colors where they mix.

Cut-out ghosts

You can use cardboard cut-out shapes to create lots of ghostly effects, like the fiery and devilish ghosts shown above.

To make your cut-out, copy the ghost shape in the pictures above onto a sheet of cardboard and then cut it out with scissors.

Fiery ghost

Put the cut-out onto a smooth surface. Place a sheet of paper over the cut-out.

Rub over the paper with wax crayons, being careful not to move the cut-out.

Color the top part again, so that the ghost appears to fade away at the bottom.

Devilish ghost

Color a sheet of paper with wax crayons, using lots of different colors.

Cover the whole sheet with a thick layer of black wax crayon. Place the cut-out on top.

Trace around the edge of the cut-out with a ball-point pen, then take it off the paper.

101

Some human ghosts

On these four pages there are lots of human ghosts to draw. Once you have tried them, you could use the techniques shown here to make anyone look ghostly.

You could turn a pop star or television personality into a see-through ghost, for example, or draw your best friend as a headless ghost…

Pirate ghost

There are lots of stories about people who have had violent deaths returning as ghosts. Unable to rest, they come to haunt the scene of their death, like the pirate on the right.

First draw this figure in pencil on a dark sheet of paper. Make it the size you want the finished picture to be.

Draw the lines shown in red. They are the basic shape of the pirate. Erase the lines shown in green.

Draw the lines shown in blue. Go over all the lines with white chalk, then add the shading.*

Draw the ghost surrounded by moonlight.

Thick chalk lines show where the moon throws most light.

Use thin chalk lines for fine details of the face and costume.

Draw the cliff with brown and green chalks. Use a thin white line for the cliff edge.

*Use a fixative spray to stop the picture from smudging.

Drawing a sheet ghost

Sheet ghosts are common in cartoons and popular around Halloween time. The idea that ghosts are like figures draped in sheets probably came about because the dead used to be buried in pieces of white cloth, called shrouds. You can find out how to draw a moving sheet ghost below.

Draw a human shape in pencil. Add a sheet around the shape with a felt-tip pen. Erase the lines shown in green.

Draw thin black lines to show how the folds of the sheet fall. Add a hint of color with a blue or purple colored pencil.

Draw the bottom of the sheet trailing to a point to make the ghost look as though it is floating. Add eyes and a mouth.

As the ghost moves forward, the head gets bigger. The body narrows into a "V" shape at the bottom.

Seeing a ghost

How would you feel if you saw a ghost? Interested or scared? As a cartoon exaggerates normal features and expressions, it is a good way to draw someone looking very frightened by seeing a ghost. Below are three steps to drawing a cartoon face.

Lines around the face and blobs of sweat show he is quaking with fear.

These are called construction lines.

Draw a circle with two pencil lines crossing in the middle.

Eyes equal distances from nose

Ears

Draw the nose where the lines meet. Add the eyes and the ears.

Drooping mouth

Erase the pencil lines and add hair and a mouth.

By making a few changes to the basic cartoon face on the left, you can show someone looking really terrified.

Go to www.usborne-quicklinks.com for a link to a Web site where you'll find stories of famous pirates, and some pictures which may help you draw them.

Headless ghost

The headless ghost of Anne Boleyn, second wife of Henry VIII of England, is said to haunt Hampton Court in London.

Anne Boleyn was beheaded in 1536.

To draw her ghost, first copy the outlines below on to black paper. Make your outline the size you want the finished picture to be.

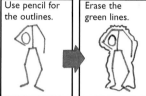

Use pencil for the outlines.

Erase the green lines.

Sketch in details of head and dress.

Doppelganger

This ghost is called a doppelganger. It is the double of a living person.

Paint a face on one half of a sheet of paper. Fold the paper in half. Press the sides together, then open them up again.

Use thick, dry paint.

Seeing your doppelganger is supposed to mean that you will die soon.

Paint the ghost with white watercolor.* You will need a thick and a thin brush.

Paint the outlines and fine details, such as the lace, with a thin, wet brush.

Use a thick brush for the folds of material. The brush should be dry and the paint so thick that it will almost not leave the brush.

Put your ghost in a setting, such as the doorway shown here.

See-through ghosts

A ghost may appear to glide through solid objects. To get a see-through effect, you can use watercolors on top of wax. Since they don't mix, anything drawn in wax will show through watercolors.

Follow these steps to draw this picture:
1. Draw the background shapes in pencil.
2. Draw the ghosts with thin wax crayons.

*You could also use white poster paint.

Genie

The story of Aladdin and his magic lamp is well known. Every time he rubs the lamp, a genie rises out of it in a puff of smoke and grants him a wish.

Use the shapes below to draw the genie.

Draw this outline very big, so that you can decorate the costume in some of the ways shown here.

Draw in the details of the face, hands and costume. Add smoke shapes around the outline.

Paint the costume with pale watercolors. Let the paint dry before you decorate the costume.

Thread spool

Polystyrene

Toothpaste lid

3. Paint a thin layer of water over the whole picture, then paint streaks of pale watercolors on it while the paper is still wet.

4. Once the paint is dry, go over the pencil lines with a thin black felt-tip pen.

Printing

You could make the patterns on the costume by dipping any of the things shown above into paint or ink, then pressing them on to the picture.

You could also use potato prints. First cut a potato in half and cut shapes into the flat edge.* Then use the cut edge to make patterns.

Ghosts from around the world

Every country has its own ghost stories and legends. Here you can see just some of the strange ghosts to be found in different countries around the world.

Ghost from Ancient China

In Ancient China, people who had been murdered were said to return as ghosts, appearing from a shapeless cloud and surrounded by green light.

To draw this picture, first copy the outlines below. Go over the finished outline with thin green and black ballpoint pens.

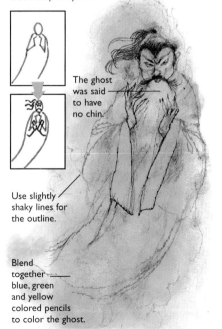

The ghost was said to have no chin.

Use slightly shaky lines for the outline.

Blend together blue, green and yellow colored pencils to color the ghost.

Japanese ghost

Use black felt-tip to go over the outline.

The Ancient Japanese believed that people who had led evil lives came back as ghosts. As a punishment for their wickedness, their legs were always in flames.

Use the outlines below to help you draw this ghost, then color it in with felt-tip pens.

*Go to **www.usborne-quicklinks.com** for a link to a Web site where you can read some spooky ghost stories. They may give you some ideas for drawings.*

Scottish kelpie

This ghost is called a kelpie, or water horse. You could copy or trace the picture, then color it with colored pencils. Use black and purple to draw the outline, and to add details to the face and coat. Use a mixture of colors to shade over the top.

According to Scottish legend, kelpies persuaded unwary travelers to ride them across a river. Once on a kelpie's back, travelers were unable to get off and the kelpie drowned them.

Use long lines for the mane and tail.

Egyptian khu

This Ancient Egyptian ghost is called a khu. People believed it caused diseases in human beings and drove animals crazy. You can see how to draw it below.

Outline the eyes and beak in black.

Seeing this dog is supposed to mean certain death.

Phantom hound

This phantom hound, called Barquest, is said to be found near graveyards in France. Use the outline below to draw it, then color the ghost with a black felt-tip pen. Use short, wavy lines to show its shaggy fur.

First, paint a watercolor wash over the paper.* Let it dry, then copy the outlines above in pencil. Draw in the background with fine felt-tip pens and draw the ghost with a red felt-tip pen.

*See the see-through ghosts on pages 104-105 for how to paint a watercolor wash.

107

Ghost train ride

A ride on a ghost train can be a terrifying experience. Once the train moves into the tunnel, there is only one way out: forward…

On these pages, you can see how to draw just some of the ghastly things that might be lurking around the next bend in the track.

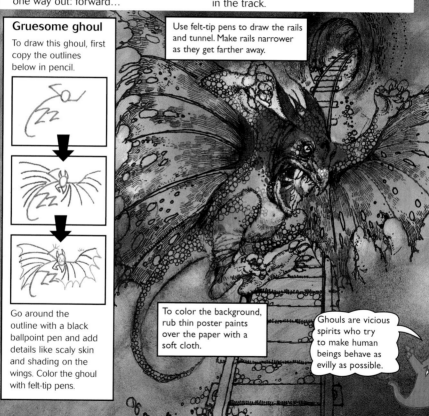

Gruesome ghoul

To draw this ghoul, first copy the outlines below in pencil.

Go around the outline with a black ballpoint pen and add details like scaly skin and shading on the wings. Color the ghoul with felt-tip pens.

Use felt-tip pens to draw the rails and tunnel. Make rails narrower as they get farther away.

To color the background, rub thin poster paints over the paper with a soft cloth.

Ghouls are vicious spirits who try to make human beings behave as evilly as possible.

Grinning skull

To draw this skull, first copy or trace the picture. Go around the outline in black and color it in with felt-tip pens.

Color the yellow areas, then add green and orange on top. Use bright colors for the slime and the eyes. Fill in the black areas and add fine details with red and black ballpoint pens.

Ghostly fiend

This hideous fiend is drawn using watercolors, ballpoint pens and colored pencils. First paint a thin layer of pale green watercolor over the page. Once the paint is dry, copy the outline shapes below on to the paint using faint pencil lines.

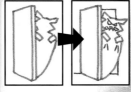

Copy details of the face and doorway from the main picture, using black, green and red ballpoint pens. Shade the doorway and the fiend's clothes with green and black colored pencils.

Cobwebs

To draw a cobweb on the wall of your tunnel, first copy the outline on the right. Draw over it with a black ballpoint pen, using shaky line strokes to suggest that the web is fragile. Add a black spider crawling out from the middle of the web.

Continue drawing the lines shown in red until your cobweb is the size you want.

Haunted houses

Everyone thinks they know what makes a house look haunted – but do they? How can you draw echoing footsteps, strange noises or sudden, icy drafts?

Here are some ideas for ways to create a menacing atmosphere and suggest an unseen, ghostly presence.

Drawing the picture

To draw the house on the right, first paint the sky across the whole page. You can see how to do it on the opposite page.

Once the sky is dry, draw the house on top and then paint it using the tips below. Finally, add the trees and other details.

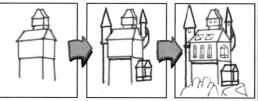

Painting the house

The picture is painted in gouache, which is a type of watercolor that professional artists often use. Its advantage over ordinary watercolors is that light colors can be painted on top of dark ones. If you don't have gouache, you could use poster paints.

The house casts lots of sinister shadows. To paint them, first copy the dark areas on the left in pencil.

Now fill them in with black poster paint. Let the paint dry, then paint the rest of the shape mid-gray. You can see how to add more detail on the opposite page.

Adding detail

The main types of brickwork are shown on the right. Use fairly thick paint for them, so that they show up well. Make sure that the original layer of dark gray paint is dry before you start.

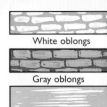

White oblongs

Gray oblongs

White lines

Gray lines

Copy the picture for more detailed shading, like that on the windows. Use pale blue to highlight parts of the house not in direct moonlight. Draw trailing plants using strokes of green paint, and add a spooky light in the window with yellow paint.

Drawing the background

The background plays a large part in creating the ghostly effect of this picture. Below are some tips to help you draw it.

For the tree, use wavy lines of brown paint. Let it dry and add white highlights. Draw flying leaves with blobs of light brown paint.

Paint the sky dark blue. Add other shades on top, letting each color dry before you add the next. When the picture is complete, draw the rain with strokes of white chalk.

You can see how to draw bats on page 117.

Inside the house

The rooms inside a haunted house may have been kept locked for hundreds of years, left exactly as they were after some terrible family tragedy.

In this picture, the outer wall has been cut away to show the inside of the haunted house. Use ideas from this picture to create your own haunted room. On pages 114-115, you can see how to draw some more strange things that you might put in the picture.

A cat senses a strange atmosphere and hisses for no apparent reason.

Light from the moon reveals a trapdoor in the floor.

A grandfather clock chiming thirteen means there will soon be a death in the family.

After years of neglect, there are cracks and cobwebs everywhere.

Bloodstains can't be removed, no matter how hard they are scrubbed.

Drawing in the floorboard lines gives a three-dimensional feel to the picture.

Adding interest

A haunted room will look more interesting if you draw the main objects in unusual positions or at unexpected angles. Put objects of different shapes and heights near each other to add variety.

Decide where the light is coming from before you start to draw. Then you can use it to create a ghostly atmosphere, by drawing lots of dark shadows, for example.

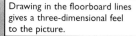

Poltergeists

Poltergeists are invisible spirits who cause chaos in a house by seeming to give objects a life of their own.

You can't see poltergeists but you can certainly see their effects. Furniture flies across the room and smashes to pieces; objects appear from nowhere; mirrors break and musical instruments start to play when no one is touching them.

Poltergeist is a German word. It means noisy spirit.

Ghostly breezes make the curtains sway, although there is no draft in the room.

The skeleton of a forgotten prisoner is slumped in the corner of a torture chamber.

You can copy this skeleton from the picture on page 98.

A secret room was used for hiding from enemies. It is reached by stairs hidden behind the fake fireplace.

Moving the front of the fake fireplace reveals a secret door.

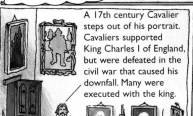

A 17th century Cavalier steps out of his portrait. Cavaliers supported King Charles I of England, but were defeated in the civil war that caused his downfall. Many were executed with the king.

Echoing footsteps can be heard and ghostly prints appear as if from nowhere.

Ghostly tale

An ancient story tells of a woman who wanted her skull built into a wall of her house when she died. Despite her wishes, however, she was buried in the family vault. Immediately afterwards, loud crashing noises, groans and slamming doors were heard. The family decided to do as she had asked. The skull was built into a wall and there was peace again.

Mix and match

Here are lots of suggestions for ghosts, vampires and frightened people to put in your drawings. Mix them in any combination you like for some really peculiar results.

See what happens when you draw a tiptoeing vampire with a chuckling ghost's head, or an angry ghost with knocking knees, for example.

Sheet ghosts

Chuckling   Shrieking   Friendly   Puzzled   Bashful   Unhappy   Angry

Waving   Threatening   Pointing   Floating by   Resting   Tripping   Dancing

Vampires*

Sly   Thirsty   Gleeful   Angry   Tired   Thoughtful   Shifty

Tiptoeing   Creeping   Climbing   Jumping   Crawling   Swooping   Lurking

*You can find out more about drawing vampires on pages 116-118.

Seeing ghosts

Shocked · Anxious · Puzzled · Alarmed · Sickly · Petrified · Disappearing fast

Wringing hands · Fingers crossed · Pointing · Walking · Tripping · Running · Quick getaway

Standing · Climbing · Knees knocking · Walking · Tripping · Running · Help!

Things to add

Sinister butler

Batty clock

Bone china

Night watchman

Bone chair

Talking heads

Deadly duo

Creepy crawly

Bat walking stick

115

Vampires

Vampires are said to be living corpses who feed on human blood. They leave the grave at sunset in search of human victims.

These pages show some of the strange ways a vampire might behave. There could be many more…

Drawing a cartoon vampire

To draw this cartoon vampire, first copy the figures below.

Copy the figure shown in green to get the body proportions right. Draw the cloak around the body and add details to the face. Color the vampire with felt-tip pens.

Draw deadly fangs for piercing victims' necks.

Add a shadow.

Vampire victim

A vampire hypnotizes its victims, so that they do not struggle and will remember nothing of the attack. Use the outlines below to help you draw this vampire victim. She is looking to one side, so the position of the features is different from the cartoon face on page 103.

Vertical construction line is curved

Line across stays the same

Eyes move around

Ears move so only one shows

Nose moves to where lines meet

Vampires return night after night until their victims die. The victims then become vampires, too.

Moving vampires

Use the green figures to help you draw these moving vampires. Fill in the body shapes around the figures.

Draw right leg bent back and left arm around face

Draw feet turned out to the side

Draw hands clasping top of cape

116

Vampire hands

Vampire hands are very thin and bony. Hands can be difficult to draw, so use the steps below to help you.

Each oval represents one joint of the finger.

Erase the ovals before adding details.

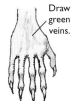

Draw green veins.

First, draw the hand as a series of oval shapes.

Next, draw the hand outline around the ovals.

Add details like the nails and the knuckles.

More hands to draw

Here are some suggestions for drawing vampire hands in other positions.

Hands are about as long as the distance from a person's chin to their hairline.

Bats

Vampires can turn themselves into bats to fly through windows and attack their sleeping victims. These bats are drawn with black and red felt-tip pens. Use the outlines to help you draw them.

Add eyes and a mouth.

Drawing a werewolf

Werewolves are human beings who change into savage, wolf-like creatures when there is a full moon. They live on human flesh and can only be killed by a silver bullet or knife. They have to be burned when they die. If they are buried they become vampires.

To draw this werewolf, first copy these outlines.

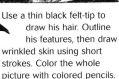

Use a thin black felt-tip to draw his hair. Outline his features, then draw wrinkled skin using short strokes. Color the whole picture with colored pencils.

117

Dracula

The most famous vampire of all is the evil Count Dracula. He first appeared as a character in a book by Bram Stoker.

Here, Dracula is about to carry out one of his ghastly attacks. Try tracing this picture, then use the tips below to color it in.

Use this outline to help you draw the part of the cloak hidden by the parchment

1. Color the outside of his cloak, his hair and bow tie with black poster paint. Use red on the inside of his cloak and top of his waistcoat, then add the red details to his mouth and around his eyes. Paint his pants gray. Let this dry, then add black stripes.

2. Color his waistcoat with colored pencils.

3. Use short, fine lines of green and black ballpoint pen to add further shading to his clothes and skin, then draw the pattern around the top of his waistcoat.

Story of Dracula

In Bram Stoker's story, Dracula lived in a huge, rambling castle in Transylvania in eastern Europe. He wanted to fill the world with vampires and planned to start in England. He traveled there by ship, killing all the crew and drinking their blood. He terrorized London with a wave of vampire attacks, but was chased back to Transylvania and killed by being stabbed through the heart with a knife.

Internet links

For more information about ghosts, go to the Usborne Quicklinks Web site at **www.usborne-quicklinks.com** and click on the number of the Web site you want to visit.

Web site 1 Phantom hounds, vampires, werewolves and other scary creatures – you'll find out all about them, and see artists' impressions and even photos on this site. Can they be real?

Web site 2 Find descriptions and pictures of some of the strange creatures in myths, legends and stories from around the world, including serpents, dragons, fairies and giants.

Web site 3 This site has designs you can print out to build a model of a haunted house. Once you have tried it, why not try designing your own?

Web site 4 Many of the creatures in this book are supposed to make an appearance on Halloween. At this site, you can find out about the origins of Halloween, and about traditions in different countries.

Web site 5 You can send a spooky e-card or download Halloween clip art and wallpaper from this site.

Web site 6 Here you'll find more seasonal Halloween clip art, and some spooky fonts to download too.

Web site 7 How much do you really know about vampires, ghosts and witches? Try the Halloween Survival Quiz at this site and find out. There are lots of other haunting puzzles and activities to try too.

Web site 8 Send your spooky stories to be published on this site, or send ideas about the things that really scare you. You can also watch the spooky Web cam, which has been set up in a haunted house, but only if you dare.

Web site 9 Join Scooby Doo and the gang in some spooky adventure games on this official Scooby Doo Web site. You'll have to collect clues and solve the mysteries along the way. Some of the games take a while to download, but be patient, as they're worth it.

Web site 10 Here you'll find a step-by-step guide to drawing a creepy vampire with evil eyes and huge, sharp teeth. Click on **Web site 11** to follow a similar step-by-step guide to drawing an ugly demon.

HOW TO DRAW
ANIMALS

Anita Ganeri and Judy Tatchell

Designed by Steve Page
Illustrated by Claire Wright
Cartoon illustrations by Jon Sayer

Additional illustrations by Rosalind Hewitt

CONTENTS

122 Drawing animals
123 Using simple shapes
124 Adding color
126 Cats and dogs
128 Horses
130 Farm animals
132 Big cats
134 Big animals

136 More wild animals
138 Bears
139 Cuddly animals
140 Water creatures
142 Countryside creatures
143 Internet links

Drawing animals

Animals may be exotic, cuddly, elegant or fierce. Some are easier to draw than others.

Cartoon pictures usually have a simple outline with exaggerated features.

Big ears

Large beak

Big eyes

If you like animals, you will probably enjoy drawing them. This part of the book shows you how to draw and color all kinds of animals in easy step-by-step stages.

Animals can make excellent cartoons. There are suggestions throughout this section for animals which work particularly well as cartoons, and for how to draw them.

Professional tips

Throughout this section, there are tips from professional animal illustrators to help you. Here are some to start.

It is easier to draw an animal if you can look at one at the same time, but this is not always possible. Animal illustrators often draw from photographs rather than from live animals.

Take a sketchbook with you if you visit a farm or a zoo. Try sketching details, such as a head or a leg, as well as whole animals.

Picture colored with watercolors and pencils

Cartoon colored with felt-tip pens

Pencil sketch

If you want to draw realistic animals, this section will help you get the shapes right. You can also see how to draw fur, slimy skin, wrinkly hide and so on.

All you need to start drawing is a pencil and paper, but there are lots of suggestions throughout this part of the book for other materials to use.

Go to www.usborne-quicklinks.com for a link to a Web site where you can see some amazing paintings and sculptures of animals, and choose a selection to create your own online exhibition.

Using simple shapes

Animals' bodies look complicated, but they are mostly made up of fairly simple shapes. In this section you can see how to draw animals using simple shapes and building up the outline around them. Here are some examples.

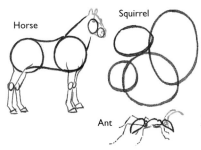

Horse

Squirrel

Ant

The shapes used to draw these animals are made up of rough circles, egg shapes, curves and lines.

Here you can see how the outlines of the animals have been built up around the starting shapes.

A horse's head

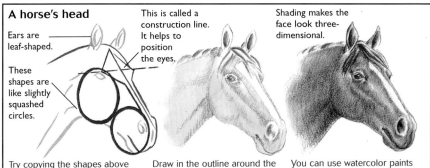

Ears are leaf-shaped.

These shapes are like slightly squashed circles.

This is called a construction line. It helps to position the eyes.

Shading makes the face look three-dimensional.

Try copying the shapes above to draw a horse's head – first the red, then the blue, then the green ones. Draw the lines in faint pencil.

Draw in the outline around the shapes and add more details to the eyes and nose. Sketch in the mane. Start to color the horse and add shading.

You can use watercolor paints or colored pencils. Here, reddish-brown and dark brown colored pencils were used over a pale brown watercolor base.

Go to www.usborne-quicklinks.com for a link to a Web site where you can see how to build up other pictures of animals from basic shapes.

123

Adding color

Animals have different types of skin, depending on where and how they live. They may have fur to keep them warm, or patterned skin for camouflage, for example.

Here you can find out how to use different drawing materials to show fur, skin, hair and so on. The ideas will help you color in the animals in this part of the book.

Furry coats

To color fur, as on this rabbit, you can use watercolor paints. Start with a smooth wash in a pale color, and let it dry. Add short, light strokes of richer and darker color for fur.

If you are using colored pencils, start by filling in the body shape with a smooth layer in a pale color. Build up the brighter and darker hairs on top, using short strokes.

For black and white pictures, use the side of a soft pencil, such as a 3B*. Press very lightly overall, then harder for shadows. Use a sharper, harder pencil, such as a 3H*, to add detail.

Short-haired coats

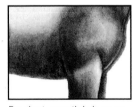

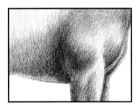

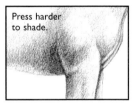

Press harder to shade.

For short, smooth hair, as on this horse, start with a pale wash. Put the main color on top, leaving pale areas for shine. Use a darker shade of the main color for shadows.

With colored pencils, you can keep the texture smooth by using blunt ones. Leave some white streaks for shine. Go over shadowed areas again, or use a darker shade.

For black and white pictures, you could use a hard pencil for the outline, then fill it in with a soft pencil for a smooth finish. You will need to "fix" pictures in pencil (see the note on page 99).

Different textures

A few lines grouped together show clumps of fur.

For long hair, as on this guinea pig, sketch faint pencil lines showing how the fur lies. Paint paler colors first, then add strokes of fur in a darker shade.

A thin, white line along the top of the body gives the skin a slight sheen.

For splotchy skin, as on this rattlesnake, start with a pale wash. Add the markings in a darker shade while the paint is still damp.

Make sure the markings on both sides match.

Butterfly wings have a delicate, powdery look. To copy this effect, you could use colored pencils or chalk pastels. You need to "fix" pastel pictures*.

Coloring cartoons

You can color cartoons in bright, flat colors. The detail is in the outline of the cartoon, and you don't need to add shadows. Use a black felt-tip pen for outlines to keep them sharp.

Professional tip

Place mask over pencil sketch.

Mask cut out of cardboard

To keep the area around your picture clean when you are painting, cut a hole the size of your picture out of a piece of thin cardboard. This cardboard is called a mask.

Place the mask over the picture and color in through the hole. You can also use the mask to test different shades of paint before you use them in the picture.

*Use a fixative spray on finished pictures to stop them smudging. See page 99 for more about fixative sprays.

Cats and dogs

The main feature of a cat's body is its very flexible spine. A dog's spine is straighter.

Here are some cats and dogs for you to draw. Can you see the differences?

A cat

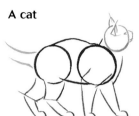

Sketch the shapes above in pencil. Start with the shapes shown in red, then the blue ones, then the green. Don't worry if you can't get them right at first. Just keep trying.

Sketch markings in pencil before you color them.

Smooth and refine the outline. Add details such as eyes, a nose and whiskers. Begin to color the cat, starting with the palest color and building the darker markings on top.

For a ginger cat use orange, yellow and brown. You could use watercolor for the base and colored pencil for the fur. Add streaks of gray to the white front and paws to show the fur.

A dog

A dog's body is leaner than a cat's.

The starting shapes for a dog are similar to those for a cat but the proportions are slightly different. The nose is longer and the body is less rounded.

Feathery streaks around the outline make it shaggy.

The dog's chest is deeper than a cat's. Its body tapers toward the back legs. You can see how the tail is really an extension of the backbone.

Adding a shadow makes the dog look as if it is standing on the ground.

To paint this English Setter, start with a pale gray, then build up darker streaks and markings on top. Leave some white streaks to highlight the long hair.

Comparing cats and dogs

Here you can see how the shapes of cats and dogs differ when they are sitting or lying down.

A cat's back is curved when it is sitting. It is curled almost into a circle when it is lying down.

It is easier to draw an animal from the side than from the front.

A dog's back is much straighter than a cat's when it is sitting or lying down.

Cartoon cats and dogs

Cartoon cats and dogs are easier to draw than real ones. Sketch your cartoon in pencil, then go over the outline with a black felt-tip pen. Color the cartoon in bright, flat colors.

Puppies and kittens have more rounded bodies than adult dogs and cats.

*Go to **www.usborne-quicklinks.com** for a link to a Web site where you can find pictures of dogs, breed information and some doggy jokes. Try drawing a few different breeds.*

Horses

Horses are fairly difficult to draw. Try the method below. Start with simple shapes and use a light pencil until the body is right. Then you can color it in.

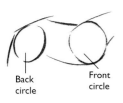

Draw two circles, one slightly bigger than the other. The larger circle is the front of the horse and the smaller one the back. Join them with curved lines to form the body.

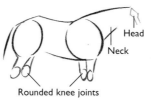

Add two tapering lines to the larger circle for the neck. Draw a narrow diamond shape for the front of the head. Draw the tops of the legs, with small ovals for the joints.

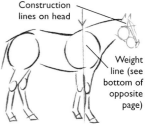

Add the ears, lower legs and the hooves. The green shapes will help you draw the head. Pencil in construction lines* to position the eyes and nose. You can erase them later.

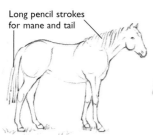

Now you can start to add more details to the basic shapes. Sketch the tail and mane in long pencil strokes. Draw the eye, nostril and mouth and erase the construction lines.

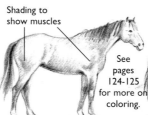

Show where the horse's muscles are with shading. Shade underneath the body too. This makes the animal look more rounded and solid (three-dimensional).

Build up the horse's color using soft strokes of colored pencil. Leave some white patches for highlights. Use a darker shade of the main color to finish off the shading.

128   *See page 123 for more about construction lines.

Horses in motion

Walking

Head held low

When a horse is walking, its front leg is lifted and the opposite back leg is the furthest behind.

Trotting

When it is trotting, the head and legs are lifted higher than in a walk. Opposite legs come forward together.

Cantering

For a canter, the head is stretched out. Opposite legs are flung out in front and behind.

A cartoon horse

Follow the stages below to draw a cartoon horse. Start with block shapes and sticks to help you get the proportions of the body looking right.

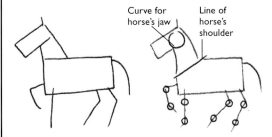

Curve for horse's jaw

Line of horse's shoulder

Round off the edges to make the outline more curvy. Exaggerate the horse's long nose, droopy lips and lumpy body. You can color it in with felt-tip pens.

Professional tip

When you are drawing an animal, it can help to draw a line which shows where the animal's weight is falling.

This is known as a weight line. It helps you to position the legs and makes the picture look balanced.

129

Farm animals

On these two pages you can see how to draw farm animals and how to turn some of them into cartoons. If you live near a farm, try sketching the live animals. You could practice the ones here first, to get an idea of the shapes.

A cow

Watercolor paint was used here.

Shallower body

Long, slender legs

Head more rounded

Weight line*

To draw a cow, pencil in the red, blue and green shapes. It has a heavier body and a shorter neck than a horse. Its neck and spine form a straighter line.

To color, shade the cream-colored areas. Then paint the bluish-black patches. When it is dry, go over the darkest areas with more bluish-black paint.

Use similar basic shapes for a calf but make them smaller. A calf's legs are longer in relation to its body than a cow's. Its body and limbs are more slender.

A cartoon sheep

Egg-shaped head

Some pale blue shading makes the sheep look more fluffy.

These lambs' legs are furrier than the sheep's.

To draw a cartoon sheep, start by copying the shapes above. The body is rectangular, with rounded corners. Draw sticks to show where the legs will go.

Draw a curly outline around the sheep's body to show its woolly coat. Draw in ears and give the face a lazy, sleepy look. Block in the shapes of the legs.

Cartoon lambs are a similar shape to sheep, but they have much smaller bodies with long necks and legs. Their legs are thicker compared with their bodies.

*The weight line is explained on page 129.

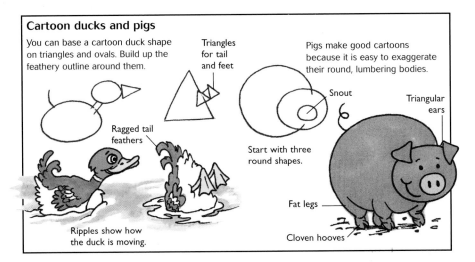

Cartoon ducks and pigs

You can base a cartoon duck shape on triangles and ovals. Build up the feathery outline around them.

Triangles for tail and feet

Pigs make good cartoons because it is easy to exaggerate their round, lumbering bodies.

Snout

Triangular ears

Ragged tail feathers

Start with three round shapes.

Ripples show how the duck is moving.

Fat legs

Cloven hooves

A hen

To draw the hen below, start with the red shapes. Then draw the hen's back, shown in blue. Then add the other blue lines and the head.

Weight line*

First, this hen was colored with a pale brown watercolor wash. The darker patches were then built up on top.

*The weight line is explained on page 129.

A rooster

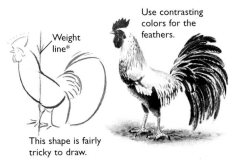

Use contrasting colors for the feathers.

Weight line*

This shape is fairly tricky to draw.

Use long curves for the rooster's body. It has a bigger comb than the hen. It also has more dramatic coloring.

131

Big cats

All cats have the same basic shape. They have long, streamlined bodies and flexible spines. Look for the differences in their head shapes and in their markings.

A tiger

The shapes for this tiger are adapted from the cat shape on page 126, but the body is longer. Start with the red shapes, then the blue, then the green ones.

Draw the outline of the tiger around the shapes. Its powerful shoulders stand out, and it has a less rounded head than a domestic cat.

To color it in, start with the lighter color and build up the markings on top. See the box opposite for more about big cats' markings.

Heads

The shapes of big cats' heads differ more than their bodies. Draw the outlines in faint pencil.

A tiger looks like a heavier version of a domestic cat, with a broad face.

Lions have long, heavy faces and chins. Only the males have shaggy golden manes.

A cheetah has a small, neat head which makes its body shape more streamlined.

A jaguar has round ears. Its mouth and nose form a pear shape.

Cartoon tiger

Start off with block shapes to draw this tiger. Use them as guidelines for filling in the body shapes. Give the tiger a big, shaggy head.

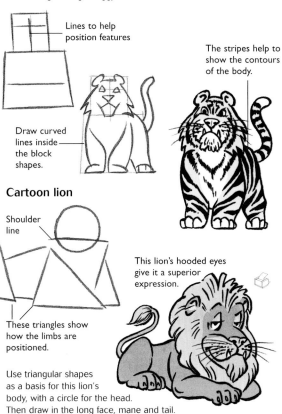

Lines to help position features

Draw curved lines inside the block shapes.

The stripes help to show the contours of the body.

Cartoon lion

Shoulder line

These triangles show how the limbs are positioned.

Use triangular shapes as a basis for this lion's body, with a circle for the head. Then draw in the long face, mane and tail.

This lion's hooded eyes give it a superior expression.

Markings

Watercolor paint was used for these markings. You could also use colored pencils.

Tiger's stripes added on top of a slightly damp, flat wash

Hairs in lion's mane added in colored pencil over a flat wash

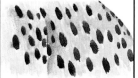

A cheetah has spots evenly spaced all over its body.

A jaguar's markings are made up of clusters of spots.

Big animals

Practice drawing tough, wrinkled hides by copying the big animals shown here.

Many big animals also make good cartoons because of their heavy, lumbering shapes.

An elephant

This is an African elephant. African elephants have larger ears than Indian elephants.

Start with the shapes above – first the red shapes, then the blue ones and then the green ones. Paint the elephant with a gray watercolor wash. Keeping the paper damp, dab on some sandy

brown patches and darker gray shadows. When it is dry, add the wrinkles. Alternatively you could use colored pencils. Keep the base colors smooth and use a sharp pencil for the wrinkles.

A cartoon rhino

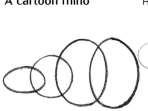

Horns Ears

To draw a cartoon rhino, start by drawing four overlapping ovals (egg shapes) for the body, as above.

Add sticks to show where the legs go. Then mark in the position of the horns and ears, as shown in red above.

You can then draw in the eyes, mouth, legs and tail. Go over the outline with a black felt-tip pen and then color the rhino.

*Go to **www.usborne-quicklinks.com** for a link to a Web site where you might spot an elephant or rhino and other amazing animals in the wild. Try drawing some of the animals you see.*

A cartoon elephant

The head is in the same position as the elephant on page 134, but the body is more upright.

A cartoon elephant looks like a simplified version of a real one. You could make your elephant look almost human by drawing it reading a newspaper or dancing, like the one above.

A cartoon whale

Start with the shape shown in red to draw a cartoon whale. Draw the whale partly submerged in the sea, squirting water out of its blow-hole. Draw its tail sticking up from below the surface.

A hippopotamus

Add the wrinkles and color the features when the rest of the colors are dry.

A hippo is a similar shape to an elephant, but it has a squattier body and stubbier legs. It holds its head down low.

Paint washes of gray and pinkish-brown. Blend the colors by "feathering"* them together.

A cartoon hippo

Try drawing a cartoon hippo based on the shapes for the real one. Emphasize its jaw and make its legs shorter and fatter.

*Blend colors by feathering while they are still wet. Dip a brush in water – don't make it too wet – and paint very delicately back and forward between two areas of color. Practice on scrap paper first.

135

More wild animals

Here are some real and cartoon pictures of grassland animals. They all have very different shapes and so will give you good drawing practice.

A kangaroo

Use very watery white paint for the highlights.

The kangaroo's weight is centered over its back legs. It uses its heavy tail for balance. After you have painted the body reddish-brown, add white highlights and dark shadows.

A cartoon kangaroo

Movement lines

To draw a cartoon kangaroo, exaggerate the huge feet, short arms and big nose. Draw movement lines to show that it is bounding along. This one has a baby in her pouch, enjoying the ride.

A cartoon aardvark

An aardvark's strange but simple shape makes it a good cartoon. This one has a long snout and big ears.

A zebra

A zebra has a similar shape to the horse on page 128. Its body is slightly shorter, though, and it has a very short mane.

All zebras are striped but their patterns can differ. Use a pencil to sketch in the markings on your zebra's coat.

Giraffes

A giraffe has plenty of features which you can exaggerate for a cartoon. Its body is a funny shape with a long neck, small head and stumpy horns.

To draw a real giraffe, start with the rough triangular shape shown in red below. Then add the shapes for the legs, the long neck and the head and tail.

Do the markings in reddish-brown first, then add a darker brown on top of the larger patches.

Color the zebra using paints or colored pencils. A zebra's stripes provide it with camouflage in long grass, so that from a distance it is hidden from hunting lions.

Professional tip

When using watercolor paints for an animal's markings, try wetting the paper first with clean water. Paint the color on while it is still damp. The different areas of color will blend together at the edges, giving a softer effect.

Bears

Here you can see how to draw three well-known types of bears. Look at pages 124-125 for some hints on how to color in fur.

A brown bear

Some brown bears stand up to eight feet tall on their hind legs. The basic shape looks very different from a bear on all fours. The bear below was colored with light brown, reddish-brown and dark brown colored pencils.

A polar bear

The polar bear is one of the strongest animals in the world. It has a rounded shape and is covered in thick white fur.

Shade the body with pale yellow and bluish-gray to make it stand out on white paper.

A cartoon panda

You can use the panda's vivid markings to make a striking cartoon. Pandas eat bamboo, so you could draw it surrounded by shoots.

Go to www.usborne-quicklinks.com for a link to a Web site where you can see how to draw more bears.

Cuddly animals

Small, furry animals look cuddly because of their size and softness. These are made up of rounded shapes.

Koala bears

This koala bear, with her baby on her back, is climbing a eucalyptus tree. Draw the shapes for the mother first and then add the baby.

Use bluish-black and brown watercolors for a soft effect.

Keep the paper damp so that the colors blend.

A baby loris

Start with the branch shape.

A baby loris has big brown eyes and long fur. Draw a faint outline, so that there are no hard edges when you color it in. Use long strokes of a darker color to make the fur look fluffy.

A seal cub

Draw the seal's body and head shape first, and then position the flippers.

Seal cubs have soft, furry white coats. They lose the fur as they grow older.

Chicks

Chicks have big feet compared with the rest of their bodies. Color the bodies rich yellow,

then use brownish-orange to shade them and to define the fluffy feathers.

139

Water creatures

Here you can see how to draw some cartoon sea creatures. You can also try some more complicated animals, such as penguins, seahorses, turtles and frogs.

A shark

Gills

To draw this cartoon shark, start with the outline above. Sharks have sleek, streamlined bodies to help them move quickly through the water. Draw the fin jutting out above the water.

Position the other fins and the gills. Draw a curve in the tail. The top part of the tail is longer and narrower than the bottom part. The shark's sharp, triangular teeth slope backward.

More cartoon fish

An octopus

Try copying the giant octopus below, resting on the sea bed. It has an egg-shaped head and eight legs covered in suckers on the underside.

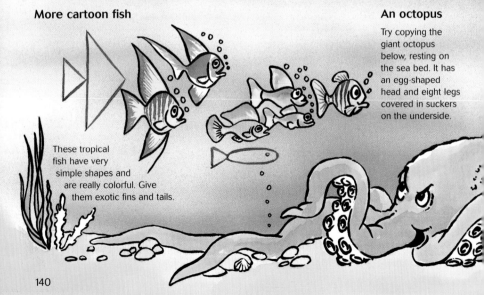

These tropical fish have very simple shapes and are really colorful. Give them exotic fins and tails.

Penguins

To draw realistic penguins, use the shapes shown on the right. Penguins' bodies are smooth and streamlined. Their small flippers make them look comical.

To paint the icy water, start with streaks of blue watercolor. Then dip your brush in water and "feather" the color outward (see page 135 for how to do this).

Add eyes when paint is dry.

Use pale shading on their fronts.

A turtle

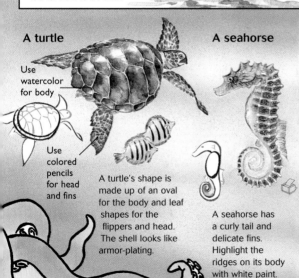

Use watercolor for body

Use colored pencils for head and fins

A turtle's shape is made up of an oval for the body and leaf shapes for the flippers and head. The shell looks like armor-plating.

A seahorse

A seahorse has a curly tail and delicate fins. Highlight the ridges on its body with white paint.

Frogs

Compare the real frog with the cartoon. The bulging eyes and wide mouth are made more prominent in the cartoon.

141

Countryside creatures

On this page you can see how to draw a few animals that live in the country. They are all shy creatures, but some, such as foxes and squirrels, do venture into towns.

Rabbits

This curve helps to position the other back foot.

Make the outline soft and furry.

Cartoon paws can look almost like human hands and feet.

A rabbit's body has a soft, rounded shape. Start with the two red circles. Then add the curve for the back.

Color the rabbit pale yellowish-brown. Use short strokes of gray for fur. Add some white strokes to make it fluffy.

Rabbits have lots of features which you can exaggerate in a cartoon. Start by drawing the shapes above.

Emphasize the rabbit's long, floppy ears, its buck teeth and big feet. Give it a cheerful, smiling face.

Cartoon hedgehogs

To draw a cartoon hedgehog, start with an oval and add two more at the front, like this. Exaggerate the nose and prickles.

A cartoon squirrel

Start with the shapes on the far left to draw a cartoon squirrel. Give it a bushy tail, round cheeks full of nuts and large front teeth.

A cartoon fox

A fox's basic shape is fairly similar to a dog's. This cartoon fox has a crafty expression due to its long, pointed nose and hooded eyes.

Go to **www.usborne-quicklinks.com** for a link to a Web site where you will find a beautiful painting of countryside creatures in northwest America. Click on any animal to find out more about it.

Internet links

For links to more Web sites about animals and how to draw them, go to the Usborne Quicklinks Web site at www.usborne-quicklinks.com and click on the number of the Web site you want to visit.

Web site 1 This "zoo without bars" has amazing photographs of animals and birds in their natural environment. Select an animal or bird from the list at the top of the page to see a picture and read more about it. Use the pictures to help you draw your own.

Web site 2 Find more animal pictures on this Web site, and watch animal movies and hear animal sounds.

Web site 3 On this Web site you can find beautiful detailed drawings of hundreds of animals, birds and reptiles. See how you can show all kinds of different textures just by using pen and ink.

Web site 4 Clear, step-by-step guides for making detailed and realistic pencil drawings of ocean, rainforest, desert and grassland animals. There are also tips for looking after your finished artwork.

Web site 5 Learn how to draw over twenty cartoon animals step-by-step. You can even have drawing tips e-mailed to you directly each week.

Web site 6 Animals' colors and patterns can help them hide from other hunting animals or humans. This site explains how to create camouflage pictures, and has links to camouflage puzzles.

These five organizations have great sites for anyone interested in animals, with pictures or photos you can use to draw from, too:

Web site 7 This online animal newspaper features a different creature every week, and has a huge archive collection of previous features. Look out for drawing competitions!

Web site 8 This site has animal news, features, fun and games, with links to Web cams. You can watch live pictures of alligators, polar bears, rhinos, tigers and other animals in zoos around the world.

Web site 9 You'll find more news here, with quizzes and lots of links to other animal Web sites.

Web site 10 This site features conservation news, photographs and information about endangered species. For the special kids' activity site, click on **Web site 11**.

Web site 12 Find pictures and facts about endangered species, games, quizzes and more fun stuff, including screensavers.

HOW TO DRAW
PEOPLE

Alastair Smith

Edited by Judy Tatchell
Designed by Nigel Reece
Illustrated by Doriana Berkovic, Derek Brazell,
David Downton, Nicky Dupays, Non Figg, Kevin Lyles,
Jan McCafferty, Paddy Mounter, Louise Nixon,
Graham Potts and Chris West
Photographs by Jane Munro Photography
Consultant: Richard Johnson

CONTENTS

146 Drawing people
148 Heads and faces
150 Drawing bodies
152 Using models
154 Pen portraits
156 Dramatic pictures
158 People in perspective
160 Fashion illustration
162 Using color
163 Collage
164 Caricatures
165 Computer cartoons
166 Body parts to copy
167 Internet links

Drawing people

Drawing people is tricky because bodies are made up of so many different shapes. This section is designed to help you draw lifelike pictures by following simple steps.

Later in the section, you can also learn how to draw caricatures and fashion illustrations. These pages contain tips on how to get started and advice on which materials to use.

● Get people to pose as models for you to draw. This enables you to check the sizes and shapes of their bodies while you draw them. If you cannot find a model, try copying a photo.

● Always plan a drawing by making a rough sketch in pencil. This way you can ensure that the whole picture fits on your paper. Get the shapes right before you draw details.

● Draw big, rather than small. By doing this, you will be less likely to draw cramped-looking pictures and you will find it easier to add details.

● Keep a sketchbook and pencil with you. Whenever you get a chance, make sketches in it. Keep old sketchbooks, so that you can look back and see how your skills have progressed.

Go to www.usborne-quicklinks.com for a link to a Web site where you will find tips on keeping sketchbooks.

Materials

It is best to color your pictures with the materials that you find easiest to use. However, you might like to try using a range of materials. This picture shows how different effects can be created by using different materials. All the materials shown here are used in the projects throughout this section.

Watercolors

Watercolors are a versatile material. You can control the strength of color, depending on how much water you add when you mix them.

When mixed with only a little water, they can look strong and vivid, like this part of the boy's sweater. When mixed with a lot of water, the colors can look watery and soft, like the middle section of the jeans.

Gouache

Gouache paints are useful for creating flat areas of color. Poster paints give a similar effect and are cheaper, but the range of colors is narrower.

Pencils

Pencils are available with a range of leads, from hard to soft. Medium leads (called HB) are ideal for rough sketching.

You will see a rough pencil sketch on page 152. There are examples of more detailed pencil drawings on page 166.

Colored pencils

Colored pencils can be used to create a range of effects. For instance, smooth, delicate shading helps to create a natural look, as shown on page 148. Page 161 shows how they can be used to create a very stylized effect in fashion illustration.

Felt-tip pens

Felt-tip pens are used for unreal styles, such as caricatures (page 164). Page 154 has some alternative ideas.

Heads and faces

Faces are the most expressive part of people's bodies, but they can be very tricky to draw. Try following these simple steps to create a lifelike portrait.

A face from the front

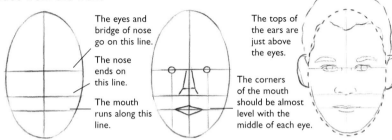

The eyes and bridge of nose go on this line.

The nose ends on this line.

The mouth runs along this line.

The tops of the ears are just above the eyes.

The corners of the mouth should be almost level with the middle of each eye.

Start by sketching an oval shape with a pencil. Then draw construction lines on it, as shown above.

Plot rough shapes around the lines in pencil. Use these shapes as guides to help you sketch the features.

When you have drawn all the lines and shapes, start sketching the features. Draw the hair as a single shape.

This picture was done with colored pencils.

Swirls of dark color were added to the hair.

Color the face and hair in a pale color. Start to build shape with more of the same color.

Instead of drawing hard lines around features, give them shape by adding shadows.

Use darker colors for areas in deep shadow. Slowly add color until the face looks rounded.

148

Artist's tip

For practice, try drawing
and shading features on
their own, in close-up.

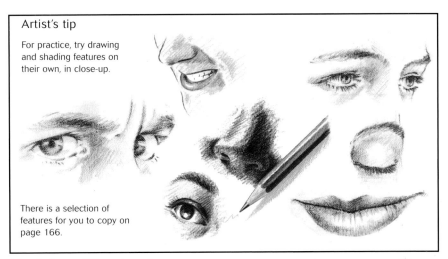

There is a selection of
features for you to copy on
page 166.

Heads from different angles

The shapes here show you
how to vary the construction
lines in order to draw heads
from different angles.

For raised and lowered
heads, use curved lines to
help you draw features in
their correct positions.

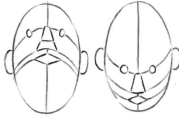

A drawing from
the side is called
a profile.

A drawing from this
angle is known as a
three-quarter view.

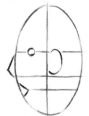

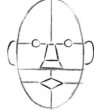
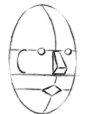
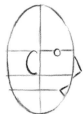

Drawing bodies

When drawing people, it is just as important to get their body proportions* right as their facial features. You should also look closely at the way they stand and what clothes they are wearing.

Start by doing some rough pencil sketches. Using the technique described below, plot the body shapes and positions carefully before drawing them in any detail.

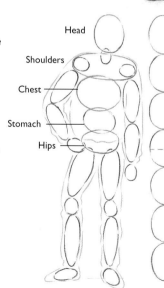

Rough sketches

Rough sketches should be done in pencil, using shapes like those on the right. Before you start, try to imagine the body parts below the clothing. This will help you see how the clothes hang when you draw them.

Start your sketch by drawing the main body shapes shown in red, then the limb shapes shown in blue.

Don't stop to erase your mistakes. Just continue sketching lightly until you think that the overall body shape looks correct. Then draw the clothes outline, shown in green.

Head

Shoulders

Chest

Stomach

Hips

To make sure the body parts in your sketch are in the right proportion, see how many head-sized ovals make up the overall height. If you are drawing an adult man, your subject will probably be about seven heads tall.

Try doing rough sketches of some of the people at the top of this page. The more times you practice drawing body shapes like these, the easier they will become.

150   *When you are drawing a person, "proportion" means the size of one part of the body compared to another.

Difficult angles

When a person is shown from a difficult angle, like the woman above, notice how some body shapes hide others. For instance, the head covers part of the shoulders, while the left arm hides the right arm.

Draw parts that are closer to you over those they cover up. Erase the parts that are covered.

Notice how the main body parts look as if they are squashed into each other.

How many heads?

People's proportions depend, for instance, upon what age they are and whether they are male or female. This guide shows some average proportions.

Women are about six and a half heads tall.

People in their mid-teens are about six heads tall.

Four year olds are about three and a half heads tall.

Shading clothes

The folds and creases formed on clothes can make them difficult to draw.

Most folds occur at joints, like the knees and elbows. Shadows are formed where folds dip inward (such as on the elbows of this coat). Highlights form where folds catch the light. Highlights and shadows are usually curved, because they form around the body.

When you draw clothes, sketch the clothes shapes over body shapes. Then sketch folds lightly in pencil before applying any color.

Leave the highlights white and build up layers of color over the rest of the garment. Add dark lines and patches to complete the shadows.

151

Using models

Artists often get someone to pose as a model for them when they draw. This helps because it gives the artist time to concentrate on the shapes a body makes in a particular position. Ask people you know to model for you. This page has tips on positioning poses. Opposite you can see how to transform your model dramatically.

Model positions

Position your models so that they are comfortable, or they will not be able to hold a pose for long. Try to make sure that they do not have to pose for more than 15 minutes at a time.

Start by drawing a rough sketch. Concentrate only on making the shape and proportions look correct. Make your sketch look about as finished as the one shown here. Do not stop to erase mistakes.

As you make your sketch, notice how the parts of the body fit together. Include the hidden body shapes in the sketch, to help you draw the model in the correct proportions.

More poses

You could try sketching these poses, or you could get someone you know to model in positions like them. Talk to your model while you sketch, to keep them from getting bored.

Transforming a model

Some artists use their sketches of models as bases for other pictures, complete with different clothes and a new background. You could use images from magazines, movies and books to give you ideas on how to transform your models.

Skydiver

To provide the basis for the drawing on the right, the model lay on the floor with his feet close to the illustrator, as shown in the picture below. The clothing and equipment were then copied from a photograph of a skydiver.

You could include the parachute canopy in the background.

To make the body look as if it is coming toward you, make the shading stronger as it gets closer to the feet.

Foreshortening

The angle of the picture above makes the feet look as if they are bigger than the head. The body and legs look squashed. This distortion is called foreshortening. On the right is another example. Drawing foreshortened people can be tricky, so always look very carefully at your chosen subject.

As this person's arm raises, the distance between the raised hand and the body looks squashed.

153

Pen portraits

Page 148 showed you how to draw the face in basic form. In this project you can now move on to create bold portraits using pens. Below are tips on which pens to use and what effects you can create with them.

Different pens

You can buy special art pens, but you can draw with any kind of pen on most kinds of paper. Experiment with ballpoint and fountain pens as well as art and felt-tip pens.

Ballpoint pen – produces a thin, even line.

Fountain pen – can be used with different kinds of ink.

Felt-tip pen – good for adding color.

Art pen – gives a smooth, controlled line.

Pen techniques and shading

Pen drawing

Unlike pencil, pen strokes don't get lighter or darker, or blend together. You can create shaded effects in pen by varying how many marks you make; more marks closer together look darker. You can leave highlights blank.

Pen drawing with smudged shading

Most felt-tip pens smudge when they get wet, because their ink dissolves in water. You can use this effect to create smudged shading by painting over a drawing with a brush dipped in water. You can see how on the opposite page.

Pen drawing painted with watercolors

Ballpoint pens and some art pens contain permanent ink (ink that won't dissolve in water). Use these pens if you want to paint over your picture without it smudging. This kind of ink stains, so be careful not to get it on your clothes.

Go to www.usborne-quicklinks.com for a link to a Web site where you will find some great tips on drawing self portraits.

Self-portrait with smudged pen

1. Looking closely in a mirror, draw your face in black felt-tip pen on thick, white paper.

2. Draw the basic shapes of your features, but don't add small details or shading.

Use a soft paintbrush and be careful not to drip.

3. Dip a brush in water. Paint over your pen lines to dissolve the ink, starting with the hair.

4. As the ink dissolves, spread it out with your brush to fill in the darkest areas of the hair.

5. Dip your brush in water again and spread the ink out further for the mid-tones.

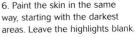

6. Paint the skin in the same way, starting with the darkest areas. Leave the highlights blank.

155

Dramatic pictures

A picture can look dramatic if it captures movement, like the drawing on the right. Another way to make a picture look dramatic is to draw it from an unusual angle, like the one at the bottom of the opposite page.

High-speed skier

The skier's clothes are colored with streaks of colored pencil to make it look as if she is traveling very fast. Most of the clothes' colors are bright and warm. When used on this subject, they help convey a feeling of danger and excitement.

Building the color

Begin by shading the lines fairly far apart. Leave highlighted areas with hardly any lines.

Build up color in darker areas by drawing the lines closer together.

Add darker shades over light shades to create shadows. Areas of light and dark make the body look solid.

The warm-colored clothes stand out against the cool-colored background. (There is more about warm and cold colors on page 162.) Color the subject first and then choose a suitable contrasting color for the background.

Mystery

Lighting can make a picture look dramatic. To make a person look mysterious, like a prowling spy, shine a single light on them from the side.

A light shone from the side is called a sidelight.

To look threatening, the model tilted his head and frowned.

Clothes are also used to set the atmosphere in this picture. Here, the subject is shown in a coat with a turned-up collar, to make him look suspicious.

Paint in black and white, with touches of light gray. To make shadows very dark, mix your black paint with hardly any water.

Unusual angles

In this picture a dramatic angle is used to add excitement: the awkward angle emphasizes how steep the drop is and the cars below almost look like ants.

Details are important here. Facial expressions highlight the person's grim determination to hang on and the leg positions suggest that he is swinging from the ledge.

Notice how the man's hands look enormous in relation to the rest of his body. This distortion is known as foreshortening. You can learn more about it on page 153.

People in perspective

Perspective drawings are based on the fact that the further away things are, the smaller they look. Things in the background are made to look as if they are the right size and in the correct position, compared with things in the foreground. On the opposite page, notice how the railroad track, trees and people all look smaller as they get further away. The railroad track disappears at a point (called the vanishing point) in the middle of the picture. Nothing is visible beyond the vanishing point.

Sketching a scene

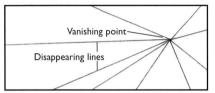

Start by drawing the vanishing point. Next, sketch guide lines (called disappearing lines) from the vanishing point. They will help you draw distant things in proportion to things that are close up.

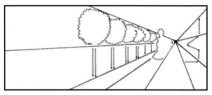

Sketch the main features of the scene using the disappearing lines as guides. In the picture on the right, the buildings, railroad track and trees have all been sketched in this way.

People in a line

When showing people in a line, directly behind each other, sketch the closest person first. Draw disappearing lines from the person's feet and head. Position the people behind inside these lines.

People not in a line

For people not directly behind one another, sketch an upright line inside the disappearing lines, level with where you want another person to go. Draw horizontal lines across from this, where the lines meet.

Go to **www.usborne-quicklinks.com** for a link to a Web site where you can learn more about vanishing points and perspective.

Creating depth

This action-packed scene was drawn using a comic-strip style. The unfinished parts should help to show you how it was constructed.

There are tips dotted around the page which show several ways to create an impression of distance in your picture.

In a realistic picture, colors get paler toward the horizon. Comic coloring is usually simpler though, so here the same colors are used in the foreground and the background.

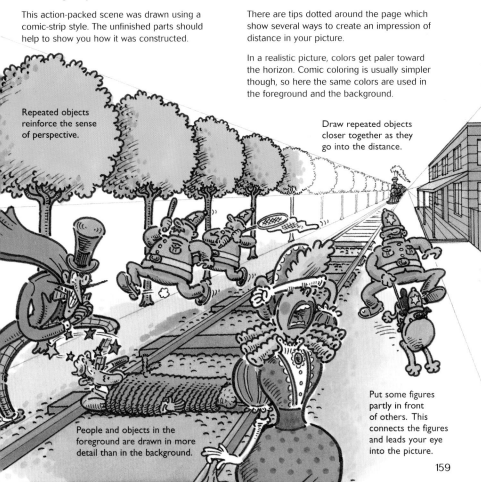

Repeated objects reinforce the sense of perspective.

Draw repeated objects closer together as they go into the distance.

People and objects in the foreground are drawn in more detail than in the background.

Put some figures partly in front of others. This connects the figures and leads your eye into the picture.

159

Fashion illustration

Fashion illustrators draw people in styles which make clothes look as glamorous as possible. They usually base their illustrations on elegant figures that are at least eight heads tall.

Sketching the pose

First, sketch a posing model. You could base your sketch on a photo from a fashion magazine. Show the proportions of a real person.

To make the figure look more elegant, lengthen the body shapes, especially the arms and legs. Make the whole body unnaturally long.

Draw the simplified outlines of clothes over the body sketch. Keep the outline sleek and flowing.

Coloring the sketch

To turn your rough sketch into a watercolor picture, like the one on the left, follow these easy steps:

1. First, color the skin tones and hair color. Mix your paint with a lot of water, for a soft, natural look. Color shapes like the knees with slightly darker tones, using a minimum of detail.

2. For the clothes, mix the paint with only a little water. Use bold brushstrokes and don't add any detail. Exaggerate highlights by leaving large areas of white (as on the left leg). Paint simplified shadows on top of the clothes.

3. When the clothes and skin colors have dried, add dark outlines to the picture, as shown. Try to paint these with single brushstrokes so the body shape looks fluid and curved. Add dark lines to the hair to give it texture.

4. When the paint is dry, add details (like facial features and earrings). Sketch them in pencil and then go over them with a fine pen.

The face of fashion

This project uses colored pencils to create a style of drawing often used in fashion design. Take a look through some fashion magazines; you could base your drawing on a photo from a magazine.

1. Draw an oval in light blue pencil. Don't press too hard. Add the features. Try drawing the eyes looking to one side.

2. Draw the hair in pale blue pencil. Draw around the sides of the face and on one side of the nose in brown. Add eyebrows.

3. Sharpen the brown pencil and add the upper eyelashes. Draw in the colored parts of the eyes with a sharp pencil.

4. Lightly shade the face in light brown. Add some darker brown down one side of the face and under the chin.

Add pink touches to the cheeks.

5. Shade the lips in pink. Add brown on the top lip, to make it darker. Color the hair with long, flowing lines.

Go to www.usborne-quicklinks.com for a link to a Web site where you can explore the world of fashion.

Using color

The colors you use will affect the mood of a picture. You can make the mood more obvious by drawing and coloring in a particular style.

Baggy suit

This jazz trumpet player is wearing a 1940s baggy suit. The drawing style emphasizes the size and bagginess of the suit, while the colors suggest the atmosphere of a dimly-lit jazz club.

Felt-tip pens were used to create strong, simple blocks of color. These blocks give the picture a bold feel.

Notice how all the shapes look angular, especially at the shoulders, elbows and knees.

Cold and warm colors

Colors are sometimes described as cold or warm. This is because people associate certain colors, such as blues and grays, with cold things, such as steel or the sea. They associate oranges, yellows and reds with warm things such as fire and the Sun.

Drawing the figure

Sketch the rough body shapes first, in pencil. Notice that there is a smooth curve from the head to the feet.

Draw lines where the clothes fold. You don't need to draw every crease. Just show the most obvious lines in the clothing.

Use the fold lines to help you divide your drawing into areas of different shades. Keep the shapes of these areas simple.

Cold colors   Warm colors

Collage

In a collage, pieces of colored paper are cut out and glued down instead of using paints. For a stylized effect, the shapes should be cut with jagged edges.

Building the collage

Make a sketch of somebody from life – an action pose works well. Lengthen the body shapes, as you would do for a fashion illustration. Add clothes shapes to the sketch.

Trace the final shapes onto colored paper. Cut out the tracings, making your cuts as straight as possible.

Glue the pieces onto a fresh piece of paper or cardboard. Then follow the tips on the right to create a finished collage.

For details, such as the white stripes on the shorts, stick smaller pieces of paper on the larger pieces.

Sketch the body and facial features over the stuck down paper, using simple, flowing lines to create the shapes.

Paint over the sketched lines with black watercolor, mixed with a little water. Use a thin brush and paint with light, fast sweeps of the brush.*

You can paint a variety of thick and thin lines, depending on how hard you press with the brush.

A colored patch behind the figure suggests the background.

As an alternative, you could use a felt-tip pen to emphasize the shapes.

163

Caricatures

Caricatures deliberately overstate a person's features to make them look funny. The best ones also manage to highlight the subject's personality. This page will show you how to make your own caricatures.

Before you start drawing, imagine the person that you want to caricature. Remember which features make the strongest impression in your mind. Make those features stand out.

Features like glasses, bushy hair, braces, big boots and a confident stance make this subject ideal for a caricature. Follow the steps below to create your own.

Building a caricature

1. Start by tracing or copying a photograph of the subject, in pencil. Without adding any detail, do a simple line drawing, making sure you include the important features of the original picture.

2. Once you have done a simple drawing, decide how you want to alter your subject. You might like to make the boots bigger and the waist skinnier, for example.

3. Try shrinking and enlarging features. To enlarge a feature, trace slightly outside the lines of your drawing (for example, see the hair below, left). To shrink a feature, trace inside it.

4. When the figure has been exaggerated enough, do a final drawing and go over the outline with a fine pen. To complete the picture, as below, use bright felt-tip pens to add color.

Make sure the original subject can still be recognized in the final drawing.

The hair is bushier.

The glasses have grown.

The belt is bigger.

The boots are huge.

*Go to **www.usborne-quicklinks.com** for a link to a Web site where you'll find tips on how to draw cartoon faces.*

Computers cartoons

This project shows you how you can use a basic drawing package, called Microsoft® Paint, to create a cartoon-style face, using simple lines and shapes. The tool symbols shown below are from Paint but they will look similar in most drawing packages.

1. Click on the **odd-shape tool** (top right). Draw a rectangular head with a pointy nose. Add a bow-tie and a triangular mouth.

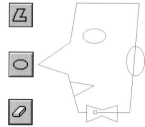

2. Use the **oval tool** (middle) to add an eye and an ear. Then click on the **eraser tool** and erase the lines inside the bow-tie and ear.

3. Select the **paint can tool** and a color. Fill in the face. Fill in the mouth and bow-tie in different colors. Leave the eye white.

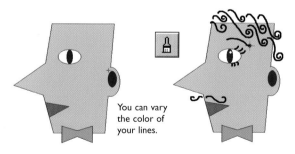

You can vary the color of your lines.

4. Click on the oval tool and select a color. Draw small ovals inside the eye and ear, and fill them in using the paint can tool.

5. Click on the **brush tool** and a color. Draw curly hair, eyelashes, an eyebrow, and a moustache. Click on white. Draw a highlight on the eye.

6. Fill in the background with the paint can. Click on the **airbrush tool** and on red. Add touches of red on the nose and cheeks.

Go to www.usborne-quicklinks.com for a link to a Web site where you can learn how to draw whole figures on your computer.

Body parts to copy

Many people spoil a well-proportioned picture by making mistakes when they draw the features in detail. To avoid this problem, try to sketch close-ups of features as often as you can, drawing them from life or photographs. You could copy the body parts on this page for practice. Don't color them in – just concentrate on getting the shapes, highlights and shadows right.

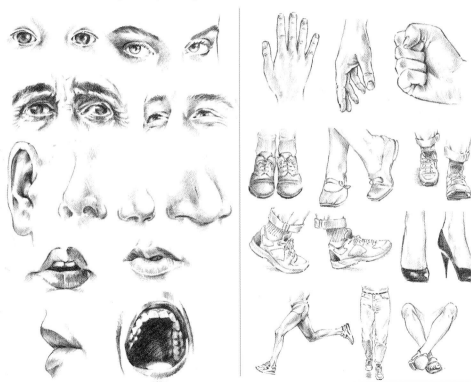

*Go to **www.usborne-quicklinks.com** for a link to a Web site where you'll find more tips on how to get individual features right.*

Internet links

For more information about drawing people, go to the Usborne Quicklinks Web site at **www.usborne-quicklinks.com** and click on the number of the Web site you want to visit.

Web site 1 This site has an easy-to-follow introduction to figure painting and tips on how to draw people in action.

Web site 2 Once you've learned the basics of figure drawing, you can visit this site, which shows you how to make an action figure flipbook.

Web site 3 Here you'll find some useful tips and tricks on how to position the features well in a portrait.

Web site 4 If you were interested in the cold and warm colors technique on page 162, you can learn more about how artists use color to create 'moods' in pictures at this site. Click on **List of Activities**, at the top of the page, then choose **Seeing Red, Feeling Blue?**

Web site 5 At this site you can see how a professional illustrator built up a drawing of a small boy, using colored pencils and ink. Click on **how I work** to access the tutorial, and then click on **next** to follow the seven steps.

Web site 6 If you're interested in becoming a cartoonist, then it's worth visiting this site where you'll find lots of practical advice. You can find out what the job of a cartoonist involves, from learning the basics of drawing to the challenges of creating a daily comic strip.

Web site 7 At this site you'll find an Online Face Maker, which you can use to create fun, cartoon faces. There are a variety of eyes, noses, mouths and other features to choose from. Click and drag the features onto the basic face shape.

Web site 8 Once you're feeling confident about drawing people, why not attempt a portrait of your whole family? You'll find lots of tips on painting family portraits at this site. Click on **A family portrait** to access them.

Web site 9 At this site you'll find lots of useful tips and ideas on how to draw figures in action.

Web site 10 Everybody has their own heroes, all for different reasons. People do courageous things every day. Why not try painting portraits of your heroes, showing why you think they're special? This Web site will show you how to. Click on **Portrait of your hero** to access it.

HOW TO DRAW
CATS

Lucy Smith

Designed by Fiona Brown
Illustrated by Chris Chapman
Additional designs by Iain Ashman
Additional illustrations by Derick Bown
Cartoon illustrations by Jo Wright

CONTENTS

170 Drawing cats
172 What to look for
174 Drawing the head and face
176 Fur and markings
178 Moods and expressions
180 Cats in action

184 Kittens and cubs
186 Big cats
188 Cartoon cats
190 Making your pictures work
191 Internet links

Drawing cats

Cats make wonderful pictures with their sleek bodies, beautiful markings and graceful, nimble movements. This section shows you how to draw all sorts, from tiny kittens to fierce tigers.

The copying method at the bottom of the page is a good way to start. It works for any picture.

Pages 178-183 show some typical cat moods and action poses.

Big cats are on pages 186-187.

Because cats spend a lot of time on the move, they are a challenge to draw well. Copying the pictures in this section will help you practice.

For kittens, see pages 184-185.

Copy cats

To start copying this cat, first break it down into simple shapes. This technique is better than simply tracing it because it helps you see how a cat's body is made up.

Tape down the edge of the tracing paper with masking tape.

Look for the shapes shown in red first, then the green, then the blue.

Flip up the tracing paper to check any details that are unclear.

Lay tracing paper over the picture and fasten as shown. Try to pick out basic shapes that make up the cat's body and draw them on the tracing paper with a soft pencil.

 Go to **www.usborne-quicklinks.com** for a link to a Web site where you can send a free cat virtual postcard or "e-greeting".

Sketching cats from life

Try to do light, flowing strokes first. You can strengthen the lines when you think they look right.

Sketch details as well as the whole cat.

Use soft pencils for quick lines.

Sketching live cats is a good way to practice watching and drawing them. As you sketch, don't stop to erase mistakes; work on getting the main lines right and keeping your strokes flowing. You can put more detail in later. Look closely at how the body is stretched or curved. Consider the angle of the head and the position of the legs and tail. It is a little more tricky to draw live big cats. You could try sketching them from a Web cam (see page 191).

Once you have figured out the basic shapes, you can make them bigger or smaller to change the size of the cat.

When you have done the outline, erase the basic shapes.

Take the tracing paper off and clean up the outline. You can either add details and color on the tracing paper, or retrace the outline onto thicker paper first.

Try copying this tiger using the method on the left and the shapes shown above right.

What to look for

This picture shows the main points to look for when drawing a cat. As you draw, try to imagine that the cat is mostly made up of simple, rounded shapes. Use smooth, curving lines to bring out its graceful build.

The head is quite small compared to the body. It is held high and forward, which helps the cat see and smell its prey when it hunts. The skull is fairly broad and rounded on top.

The spine is long and so supple that the cat can arch its back nearly double without hurting itself.

Color the eyes yellowish-green. Add darker green at the top and around the pupils. Make these solid black.

The front legs, or forelegs, are very flexible at the joints. All the cat's legs join its body high up on the skeleton, not just at tummy level. Draw them with this in mind to make the lines flow.

Cats have pointed elbow joints high up on their front legs.

The paws are oval in shape. They are only toes, not the cat's whole feet. Cats move so lightly and gracefully because they balance on their toes.

172

Most cats have tails almost as long and supple as their spines. The tail is really an extension of the spine, so try to make the two flow in a continuous line.

The hips, or hindquarters, are very muscular which is why cats can spring so far and fast. You can find out how to make them look muscular below.

These joints are the cat's heels, called hocks. They stick out backward when it is standing up, but rest on the ground when it sits.

The muscles under the skin make the curves you see on the surface. You can make a shorthaired cat, like this one, look muscular by shading faint lines in a darker color.

Drawing the cat

Using a soft pencil, draw the big ovals of the body, chest and hindquarters first, and the smaller head circle. Add the legs, paws and tail, then the face and ears.*

The line of the cat's belly is almost straight.

The legs join the body high up.

Refine the outline and erase any unwanted lines. Apply a pale grayish-blue base, but let the paper show through on the lightest parts to give a rich sheen to the fur.

Use colored pencils or a watercolor wash for the base.

Add detail to the face*: coloring the eyes helps bring it to life. Darker gray shadows give the cat form (see the tips on the right).

Professional tips

Proportions. To help you get the proportions and outline right, look at the space in between parts of the cat: for example, the shape of the space framed by the cat's tummy and legs and the space between its hind legs.

Shadows. Adding shadows to your drawing helps to make the cat look 3D and rounded. You need to shade the parts which the light does not fall on directly.

It helps to imagine the cat's body as a cylinder.

Direction of light

Direction of light

Mark arrows on your drawing to show the direction of the light. This will help you figure out which parts of the cat should be in shadow.

*You can find out how to draw a cat's face in detail on pages 174-175.

Drawing the head and face

Cats use their facial features in many ways to show their moods, so drawing the face adds real character to your pictures. Here, you can see how to structure the head. Opposite are more hints about how to draw the cat's main features in detail.

A cat's head

Use a soft pencil.

Draw a circle. Add a vertical line down the middle to help you to position the features evenly on each side of the face. Draw a small oval in the lower half of the circle for the muzzle.

Horizontal lines make sure the eyes are level.

Near the top of the oval, draw a little upside-down triangle for the nose. Draw wedge shapes out from this to the rim of the head circle, to help you to position the eyes and ears.

The ears are triangles.

The broken outline gives a furry effect.

Add the mouth as an upside-down Y-shape. Erase any unwanted lines. Color the head pale fawn, fanning your pencil or brush strokes out from the middle to follow the lie of the fur.

Shade under and around the muzzle to give it shape. Refine the outlines and, using the tips on these two pages, add detail to all the features.

To color the eyes, do a layer of yellow, then orange. Add brown shadows. If you use paint, let each layer dry before applying the next. Add the black pupils.

The nose and eyes together form a V-shape.

The mouth is small when shut, with very fine lips.

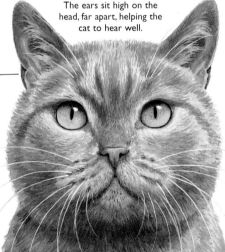

The ears sit high on the head, far apart, helping the cat to hear well.

Add tan shadows.

The eyes are big and widely spaced.

Draw the whiskers last, in white.

Eyes

The most striking things about a cat's face are its eyes. They give an immediate impression of its character. You can make the eyes look more intense by coloring them darker at the top and lighter toward the bottom. Adding a white highlight to each eye makes it look bright. Cats' pupils change size and shape depending on how much light there is. This helps them to see well.

The eyes are spheres so the highlight falls in the same place on each one.

In strong light, the pupil is a narrow slit.

In good light, it is a medium-sized vertical oval.

In dim light, it widens and is circular, filling most of the eye.

Nose

The nose is basically a small triangle shape. Do tiny dots of color very close together to build up a textured effect on the nose skin. This technique is called stippling (see page 177).

Do the nostrils darker to make them look hollow.

Whiskers

Cats use their whiskers to touch things and sense changes in the air. Most of them grow in several rows on each side of the muzzle. Only add the whiskers when the rest of the face is finished. Using a sharp, white colored pencil, do soft, curved strokes.

Do little dots where each whisker grows.

Ears

Cats have excellent hearing. Their ears are shaped like half a cone turned upside-down so they can catch sound easily.

A cross section of a cat's ear seen from the side.

There isn't any fur inside the ears and the skin is pale. But when you are drawing the ears you need to make the innermost part really dark to give them shape. Try shading along the outer edge for a 3D effect.

Add longer, lighter hairs at the edge of the ear.

Go to **www.usborne-quicklinks.com** for a link to a Web site where you can find out why cats' eyes glow in the dark.

Fur and markings

There are lots of different breeds of domestic, or pet cats, all with different fur lengths and markings, so it is worth practicing drawing fur in detail. These two pages give tips on how to get the right effect and which drawing materials to use.

Drawing different types of fur

For short fur, pick out the palest color in the coat and apply it in either light pencil or a watercolor wash (see opposite). When it is dry, add lots of short, close strokes of darker color.

Use longer, looser strokes of color for longer fur. Group several strokes together, as shown, for a tufted effect. Make the strokes flow down rather than along the sides of the body.

Rex cats have tightly curled fur. To draw it, do short, arched strokes very close together in rows over the base color. To achieve a rippling, shiny look, let the base show through in between the rows.

Common colors and markings

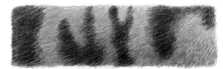

Tabby cats have pale coats with dark stripes. Start by applying the base color. When it is dry add the stripes, making them follow the curves of the cat's body (see page 180).

To draw a white cat on pale paper, use colored shading to give it shape. Try warm fawns or yellows to get a sunlit or firelit effect, or cool blues if the cat is in moonlight or shadow.

For cats with white patches, color the darker areas of the coat first, letting some white show around the edges where the dark and light hairs overlap. Then add soft shading on the white parts.

*Go to **www.usborne-quicklinks.com** for a link to a Web site where you can find out how to draw cats' fur in great detail.*

Techniques and materials

These are some examples of different drawing methods and materials which can create convincing furry effects. Use a sharp pencil or fine brush to draw single hairs.

Colored pencils

Hatching is lots of short, straight lines done side by side close together. It is good for short, sleek fur.

Cross-hatching is layers of short lines going in different directions. It gives a dark, dense look, useful for shadows.

Blocking means using the side of the pencil point to get a flat area of color with no gaps showing.

Colored pencils on a rough-textured paper give a broken, fuzzy line which is good for fluffy or long fur.

To do fine, white hairs, try scratching through colored pencil with a compass point on a thick piece of paper.

Watercolors

The damp paper helps the color blend in and gives a more even tone.

A watercolor wash is a quick way to do the first layer of color. First, mix the paint. With a soft, thick brush, wet the paper with water. Let it soak in but, while it is still damp, put plenty of color on the brush. Starting at the top of the page, do bold strokes back and forth until you reach the bottom.

Stippling. With a small, blunt brush, do masses of tiny dots of color close together. A stiff brush works well, or you could cut the tip off an old, soft one.

Stiff brush

Soft brush

For fine detail, dab a little paint on a brush and apply it in strokes over a dry wash. This method is called "dry brush".

Wet watercolor. Wet the paper and immediately apply splashes of paint for a soft, blurred effect. This makes a good base for realistic-looking fur markings.

Moods and expressions

Cats are very expressive and use their whole bodies to show how they feel. These two pages show some typical moods to draw, and there are tips on how to make them look really vivid.

Sleepy

A cat curled up like this in a cozy ball is fairly easy to draw, because the whole picture makes an oval shape.

Do triangles for the ears and slanting slits for the eyes.

In pencil do the shapes shown in red first, then the green, then the blue. Use the method on page 176 to build up the coat.

A curved, furry outline gives a peaceful, cozy look.

Use pastels or watercolors for a soft, gentle feel. A pinkish haze and orange highlights on the cat's fur suggest a fireside glow.

Aggressive

The tail is up and the back is arched.

The ears are back and out.

One front paw is poised to lash out.

A threatened cat may react aggressively like this. As you do the basic shapes, note how this pose makes the cat look as big as possible.

Short, sharp strokes make the fur look bristly.

The cat stands sideways with its fur out to look bigger.

Go over the outlines, making them bold and strong to suggest the fierce mood and to add impact to the picture. Apply pale fawn as a base.

Add the teeth using white poster paint.

Whiskers exaggerate the snarl.

The claws are out.

This splotchy coat pattern is called tortoiseshell. Build it up by adding patches of gold, rust, dark brown and black once the base is dry.

Alert

Because you are seeing this cat almost head on, you need to draw the parts closest to you bigger than the rest. To make the front and back legs look as if they are lined up behind each other, close up the gaps between them. This is called foreshortening.* To get this pose right, trace the basic body shapes carefully.

The head looks big as it is closest.

The body ovals overlap to bring the front and back legs close together.

Bold shapes make the drawing look lively.

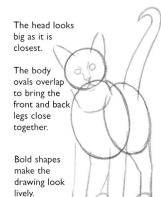

The tail is curved up like a question mark.

The ears are pricked.

The eyes are wide.

Draw the back legs shorter than the front, so they seem further away.

Frightened

Try to figure out the basic shapes of this frightened cat for yourself. Its whole body is tensed as it cowers away in terror. Notice how the fur is raised on its back.

For spiky fur, draw short, straight lines out from the middle of the body.

The back is arched.

The ears are flattened.

The tail is curved.

Relaxed

The paws are limp because the cat is very relaxed.

The pale tummy and chin are exposed.

Once you have figured out the basic shapes of this contented cat, apply a creamy-white base all over. Build up the orange markings, using long, loose lines for a supple look. The tummy and chin are exposed, so keep those areas pale. Use light gray for soft shadows and brownish-orange for deep ones.

*There is more about foreshortening on page 183.

179

Cats in action

Cats are very agile, so drawing them in action can be difficult because they move fast and get into all sorts of acrobatic positions. This page gives advice on getting a sense of movement into a drawing and on the next three pages there are action pictures to copy.

Start with some simple line sketches. If the picture looks too static, abandon it and try again. Exaggerate the lines a little to create a sense of movement.

The eyes fixed ahead give a purposeful look.

The hind legs propel the cat forward.

Once the basic lines are right, put in the body shapes as shown above. Use a soft pencil and don't press hard at this stage: keep the lines light and flowing.

Professional tip

Use the space around the cat to suggest movement, by keeping the background simple. A detailed one is distracting and slows the movement down by cluttering the picture and blurring the outlines.

Lifted paws show that the cat is in mid-stride.

Improve the outlines making them stronger and cleaner now to give a feeling of energy. Erase any unwanted marks and apply a fawn base.

The curving and stretching stripes emphasize movement in the picture.

Start to build up the russet stripes with broad strokes of watercolor. Apply individual hairs with a thin brush, using short stokes.

Go to www.usborne-quicklinks.com for a link to a Web site where you will find lots of funny photos of cats making mischief. Try drawing a few for practice.

Sharpening claws

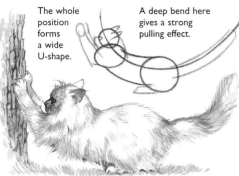

The whole position forms a wide U-shape.

A deep bend here gives a strong pulling effect.

For this picture, draw the cat before the tree. Start by doing a curved line, as shown, to get the feel of the movement sweeping through the whole body. Use the tips on page 176 to help you draw the long fur.

Washing

Cats have such supple spines that they can bend almost double, like this, to wash their hindquarters. This position looks hard to draw because it is so contorted, but the basic shapes are fairly simple.

The hind legs form a V-shape.

The spine is curved almost into a circle.

Fighting

Try copying this picture, using the method on pages 170-171 to discover the basic body shapes. The tips here will help you position the cats.

The back is parallel with the dark cat's left foreleg.

This cat is protecting itself. Its body is off-balance and its legs and tail stretched taut.

For this cat, use bold curves to show how its whole body is coiled and arched ready to spring forward.

Jumping up

Cats can jump up to four or five times their own height. For this dynamic picture, draw the Siamese cat's body stretched out to its fullest extent. As you put in the shading, add a shadow on the ground. This shows that the cat is high in the air.

Draw the paw in contact with the ball, to show that the cat is in control of it.

A background of sky with no ground visible suggests the cat is high up.

The cat is looking up, focusing on where it wants to land.

Jumping down

Because this cat is jumping down, its body is stretched straight out to shorten the distance it has to drop. Do a long oval for the main part of the body to emphasize the stretch. Notice that the chest and thigh ovals are parallel, showing how the cat has balanced itself perfectly for the leap. Its back legs are folded ready to push it off into the air. Drawing the cat from a low angle makes it seem as though it is high up.

The hind legs are long and taut. Add shadows for definition.

The tail is up and out to help the cat balance in the air.

Add chocolate brown to the ears nose, tail and paws.

182

The eyes are fixed on its prey.

Use bluish highlights as the moon casts a cold, eerie light.

Draw in the slope when you do the basic shapes, as it affects the way the legs are positioned.

The whole position forms an S-shape.

The stalking cat would look like this from the side.

Stalking

Cats crouch down low like this to stalk their prey. You need to use foreshortening here because the cat is coming toward you. The parts you cannot see are still there, but hidden. Cats often hunt at night, and this moonlit background adds suspense to the picture. The moon is the light source, so put it in before you color the cat to see where to shade and highlight the fur.

Stretching

Cats almost always stretch their whole bodies like this just after waking up. When you have drawn this cat, add a long, thin shadow under as shown to increase the stretched look.

The lifted forepaw gives a sense of movement.

This smooth curve gives a supple feel.

Kittens and cubs

Kittens make cute, lively pictures. They are pretty hard to draw, though, because their bodies are softer with less definite lines than adult cats'. They also have different proportions.

Four-week-old kitten

The ears are very small and rounded.

Blunt muzzle

The eyes, nose and mouth are close together.

The tail is short and pointed.

Nine-week-old kitten

At this age, the ears are long and pointed.

The basic body shapes are very round.

Very young kittens, like these, have big heads in relation to their bodies. Their legs are fairly short and thick, with big paws. Kittens look cuddly as their fur is very soft. For a fluffy look, blur the outlines so there are no hard edges.

A nursing cat and kittens

The cat and kittens form a fan-shape.

The kittens' heads and bodies overlap. The legs and paws are tucked away.

The wriggling tails add a lively touch.

The closed eyes give the cat a contented look.

For this picture, position the mother cat before starting on the kittens. Use her front and back legs to help you put each kitten in the right place.

Use smooth, flowing lines to create a peaceful feeling. The cat's body is long and loose, but the kittens are rounded and tightly packed together.

Their different colors and markings also add interest. For each one, do the palest colors first then add the patches and stripes using soft strokes.

Kittens at play

When kittens aren't eating or sleeping, they spend most of their time playing. Try copying the mischievous pair below and the inquisitive tabby kitten at the bottom of the page.

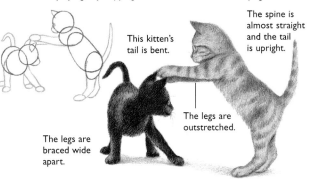

This kitten's tail is bent.

The spine is almost straight and the tail is upright.

The legs are outstretched.

The legs are braced wide apart.

Draw the black kitten first. It is seen from the front, so you need to use foreshortening (see page 179) to get it right. Its body is low and tense, ready to spring.

To position the tabby kitten, look at the space between the two animals. The tabby's body is parallel with the line of the other's left foreleg.

Its eye is fixed on the ball.

There is a smooth curve from the spine to the tail-tip.

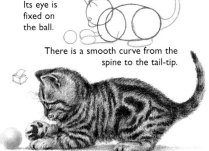

For this crouching position, draw the head and body shapes close together. Make the tabby stripes crinkly to give the body a compressed, coiled look.

The taut whiskers and flicked-up tail give the kitten a playful feeling.

Cubs

Like pet kittens, baby big cats (cubs) look different from adults. Compare these lynx and cheetah cubs with the adults on page 187.

A lynx cub's ears are very long with tufted tips.

The cheeks haven't grown long fur yet.

The huge legs and paws make the cub look gawky.

A cheetah cub's head and face are more rounded than the adult's.

Fluffy coat

185

Big cats

With their dramatic markings and powerful, elegant bodies, big cats make striking drawings. Although their size and coloring make them seem very different from pet cats, in fact most have similar body structures.

Tiger

The tiger is the biggest of all the cats. It has a heavy head and body set on thick, strong legs. Try painting it with pale yellowish-brown watercolor. Let this dry, then add reddish-brown as shown. While this is still damp, paint in the black stripes.

The back and neck form an almost straight line.

Add a long oval for the muzzle.

The tail is held low.

Slightly blurred stripes give a furry, rippling look.

Do thick tufts of fur here.

Lion

Lions have long muzzles, big heads and thick, powerful bodies. To color the lion, apply a pale, sandy base all over, then apply a mixture of gold and reddish-brown on top. Leave the chin white and add whiskers in white colored pencil.

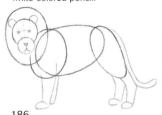

Use similar shapes to the tiger, but with bigger, rounder ears and an outer oval for the mane.

Do the rich, brown mane last, over a sandy base.

The lion in this picture is looking straight at you, giving the picture a strong focus.

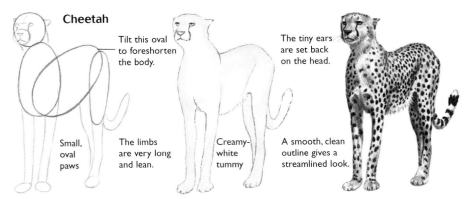

Cheetah

Tilt this oval to foreshorten the body.

The tiny ears are set back on the head.

Small, oval paws

The limbs are very long and lean.

Creamy-white tummy

A smooth, clean outline gives a streamlined look.

Unlike other big cats, the cheetah's body is similar to a dog's. The ribcage is deep and the tummy tucks up under the hind legs. In pencil, draw the basic shapes, as above left, and refine the outlines. Notice how the skull is flatter than other cats'. Place the eyes higher up to suggest this. Apply a light, yellowish-fawn base and add shading, as shown, in light brown. Color the eyes amber and the nose and lips black. Finally, add the black spots.

Northern lynx

The lynx looks fairly similar to a pet cat. It has a short, heavy body and long legs with very powerful hindquarters. The long tufts of fur on its cheeks move according to its mood.

Copy the basic shapes on the right and refine the outline. Apply a fawn base all over. Leaving the underparts pale, color the head and upper body reddish-brown. Do soft, blotchy spots around the legs.

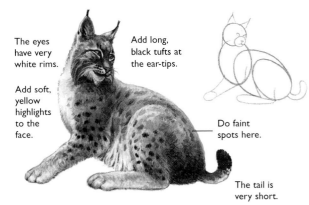

The eyes have very white rims.

Add long, black tufts at the ear-tips.

Add soft, yellow highlights to the face.

Do faint spots here.

The tail is very short.

Go to *www.usborne-quicklinks.com* for a link to a Web site where you can follow a step-by-step guide to drawing a cheetah running.

Cartoon cats

Cats' strong characters, expressive faces and their habit of getting into comic scrapes make them ideal subjects for cartoons. This page has tips on drawing cartoon-style cats. You can learn how to create lively, funny pictures full of interest and action. The opposite page shows you how to draw four different cat characters.

Cartoon cat

In pencil, start by doing the basic shapes as shown above. For a comic look, exaggerate features like the eyes, teeth and claws. Use strong, bold lines.

Zigzags make the outline look soft and fluffy.

Go over the outlines and features in waterproof black felt-tip pen, then lightly pencil in the inner edges of the markings. Try to keep all the lines clear and clean.

Leave the white markings blank and apply a light orange base over the rest. When this dries, put in dark orange stripes. To create a lively look, use bright, solid colors. Felt-tip pens or colored inks work best for a cartoon-style finish.

Add a bent whisker and a few stray hairs last, in black, to give the cat more character.

Color the eyes bright green. Add tiny, black pupils when the green is dry.

A collar and name tag add a touch of extra color and fun.

White patches on a bright coat make the cat look comical.

Give each marking a definite crisp edge for a more striking effect.

*Go to **www.usborne-quicklinks.com** for a link to a Web site where you can learn how to draw a simple cartoon cat.*

Different kinds of cartoon cats

Fat cat

Very large, round face and body.

Broad, colored patches on a white coat help to make the cat look fat.

Big paws

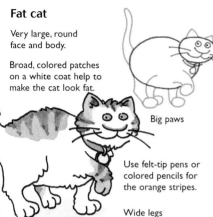

Use felt-tip pens or colored pencils for the orange stripes.

Wide legs

Smug cat

Set the eyes high up on the face so the cat seems to be looking down its nose.

Draw the eyelids half-closed.

A small, neat smile gives a smug look.

Upturned whiskers give a snooty expression.

Pale blue shading makes the white look crisp and clean.

Alley cat

A nick at the edge of one ear suggests the cat has been in a fight.

Make the whiskers bent and ragged.

A fish skeleton shows that the cat has been scavenging through trashcans.

Give the cat a big grin.

Put in the occasional zigzag for a scruffy look.

Kittens

Spiky whiskers give a lively look.

For the tabby cat on the left, apply a light brown base then add dark brown stripes.

Short, stiff, pointed tail

Tiny movement lines add energy and action.

189

Making your pictures work

Good pictures involve more than just drawing convincing likenesses. Here are two great tips on how to add a lot of impact to a picture and make it really successful.

Composition

Roughly sketch the whole triangle first, then work out each kitten's place in it before putting in the details.

The composition of a picture means the way all the things in it are arranged. Here are two ways to group four kittens into a good composition. In the picture above, the kittens form a triangle. The grouping is interesting because the kittens look so alike but are on slightly different levels. The triangle shape draws your eye along the line across each face.

This grouping also works well because it is almost symmetrical. If you folded it vertically down the middle, each half would almost mirror the other.

A good way to compose a picture is to sketch each thing you want to include on a separate scrap of paper. Then move the pieces around until they look right together.

Point of view

The angle or point of view from which you draw can add power to a scene. This prowling kitten is seen from its own eye-level. This emphasizes the kitten's wide, blue eyes, and makes a really dramatic focus.

The blades of grass show how small the kitten is: its tail hardly comes above them.

Draw the kitten first. Its body is hidden because of foreshortening, so make the face detailed as it is the focus of attention. Put the grass and flowers in last.

190

Internet links

For more information about cats and how to draw them, go to the Usborne Quicklinks Web site at **www.usborne-quicklinks.com** and click on the number of the Web site you want to visit.

Web site 1 Here you'll find a really good selection of big cat pictures to copy. Click on a title from the list, and it will be displayed on your computer screen. You can then draw directly from the screen.

Web site 2 At this site you can view the gallery of an artist who loves to draw and paint cats. Click on a "thumbnail" (small) image to see an enlargement.

Web site 3 Here you'll find a great step-by-step lesson on how to draw a crazy cartoon cat.

Web site 4 If you're interested in big cats you'll find lots of information and pictures of all the different species here.

Web site 5 Web cams show live pictures from around the world and are useful for drawing big cats. It is amazing to think that the cat you draw is roaming around in the wild at that very moment.

Web site 6 At this site about the popular cartoon "Felix the cat", you can read about the history of the cartoon, join the Felix fan club, download Felix wallpapers for your computer desktop and read some online comics.

Web site 7 You can learn about tigers at this interactive Web site where it's your job, as the zookeeper, to design the tiger enclosure for your rescued tiger.

Web site 8 Find out what you can do to help endangered tigers, or send your poems, stories and pictures of them to be published on this Web site for kids. You can also download some tiger wallpapers to decorate your desktop.

Web site 9 Cats come in all colors, shapes and sizes. One breed, the Canadian Sphynx, has virtually no fur at all. At this site you'll find pictures and information on lots of different cat breeds from around the world.

Web site 10 You've learned how to draw a cat, now learn how to draw *like* a cat. From the site's home page, click on **Draw like a cat.**

HOW TO DRAW
HORSES

Lucy Smith

Designed by Fiona Brown
Illustrated by Chris Chapman,
Jamie Medlin and Adam Hook
Cartoon illustrations by Jo Wright

CONTENTS

194 About this section
196 Drawing a horse
198 Horses' heads
200 The paces
202 A rearing horse
204 A bucking horse
205 Dressage
206 Cross country
207 A jumping pony
208 Show jumping
210 Cartoon horses
212 Different breeds
214 Pegasus
215 Internet links

About this section

Horses are both graceful and athletic, but drawing them can be difficult because of their complex body structure. In this section you can learn how to achieve the right proportions and produce some dramatic pictures.

A good way of learning how a horse's lines should flow in a drawing is to trace a picture like the one on the opposite page. You can then move on to drawing a horse from scratch using the method described on pages 196-197.

The pictures in this section use five types of drawing materials: pencil, gouache, watercolor, felt-tip pens and colored pencils. Examples of the first four are shown on the right, while the opposite page gives some tips about using colored pencils.

Pencil works well for detailed drawings, as it is easy to control. Pencils are coded according to how hard or soft they are. This head was done mainly in a soft HB, with the dark eye and mane drawn in a softer 2B.

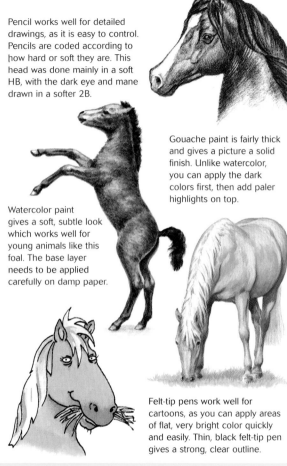

Gouache paint is fairly thick and gives a picture a solid finish. Unlike watercolor, you can apply the dark colors first, then add paler highlights on top.

Watercolor paint gives a soft, subtle look which works well for young animals like this foal. The base layer needs to be applied carefully on damp paper.

Felt-tip pens work well for cartoons, as you can apply areas of flat, very bright color quickly and easily. Thin, black felt-tip pen gives a strong, clear outline.

*Go to **www.usborne-quicklinks.com** for a link to a Web site where you will find information and tips on lots of different drawing materials.*

Tracing and coloring

Lay a sheet of thin tracing paper over this picture. Fasten it with two strips of masking tape to hold it still. Trace the image carefully with a fairly hard pencil, such as a 2H.

To transfer the image to thicker paper, turn the tracing paper over and go over the lines in a soft pencil, such as a 2B. Turn the sheet back over and lay it on the thicker paper.

Redo the outlines in harder pencil. The soft pencil on the underside will be transferred to the thicker paper. You can then refine the outlines before applying color as below.

The first layer of color should be pale. Apply either a soft watercolor wash or a thin layer of light brown colored pencil all over.

Let the base color show through on parts where the light falls. This adds shape and makes the coat shine.

Flowing strokes work best for the mane and tail. Use a gray base, with dark brown on top.

A small amount of black on the darkest parts adds the finishing touches.

Adding a slightly darker shade over the base color deepens the coat color.

Further layers of shading using dark brown colored pencil bring out the muscular parts of the horse.

195

Drawing a horse

A horse's shape is complicated, so to make your pictures look right, it is important to get the different parts in proportion. An easy way to do this is to imagine a horse as being made of simple shapes. The horse below has been broken down into basic shapes, using construction lines. Try copying it by doing the lines shown in red first, then the green, then the blue. The opposite page has tips on adding color to finish.

Draw the ears as narrow triangles.

The top line of the neck forms a smooth curve. The lower line is shorter and straighter.

The chest and hindquarter circles are the same size. They are linked by parallel, curved lines.

All the yellow lines are the same length. Use them to check that different parts of the horse are the correct size in relation to each other.

The head is made up of two ovals. There is more about drawing it on pages 198-199.

The outer edges of the buttock, hock and fetlock are in a straight line.

These are construction lines. They help you to get your initial drawing right.

The knees are small circles.

The hind legs join the body higher up than the forelegs and slope down and back to the hock joints.

These joints, called hocks, are set just a fraction higher than the knees.

The ankles, called fetlocks, are slightly smaller circles than the knees.

The hooves can be drawn as box shapes.

196

Getting a good finish

Here you can see how to complete the picture to get a realistic effect. Refine the outline, then erase the lines you no longer need before applying a pale yellow-gold as the base color.

Gradually deepen the coat color with layers of darker gold and brown. When using paint, as here, make sure you let each layer dry before applying the next one.

Forelock

The full mass of the mane is suggested by soft, curved strokes of paint, with dark, colored pencil shading separating the strands.

Highlights on the hindquarters make them look rounded and glossy. To achieve this effect, let the pale base show through.

Use a blend of long white, yellow and gray strokes to color the tail.

A long line of deep shading here creates the dark crease called the jugular groove.

Shading on the neck, shoulder and hindquarters emphasizes how muscular they are and gives a three-dimensional look.

This is a piece of bone-like material called the chestnut.

Fine, dark lines in colored pencil suggest the tendons and ligaments.

Shadows on the underside of the knees and fetlocks make them look rounded.

Horses' heads

A horse's head is its most beautiful and striking feature, so drawing it in detail can produce lovely pictures as well as being good practice. On this page you can learn how to build up the head in four stages. Opposite are a variety of different types to try. Each one has hints on how to achieve the finished look.

Stage 1

Do a large oval for the main part.

Add a small overlapping oval for the muzzle.

Stage 2

Construction lines help to position the features.

This distance…

…is almost the same as this distance.

This is about half the distance above.

Stage 3

Refine the outlines and erase the construction lines.

Apply pale gold as the base. Let the paper show through on the lightest parts.

198

Stage 4

Shading inside the ears fills out their shapes.

Using a very sharp pencil, add the fine eyelashes.

Paint the eyes black and add tiny white dots, or highlights, to make them shine.

Soft brushstrokes give a velvety look to the muzzle.

Dark shadows inside the nostrils give them depth.

Do fine gray and fawn strokes for the mane.

Add the veins as dark lines.

Palomino horses, like this one, are golden with white or flaxen manes and tails.

A pony

The eyes are placed halfway down the main oval and at the sides of the head.

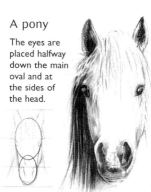

You don't need to draw every hair in the mane. Shading under it suggests a mass of thick hair.

Slightly curved lines down the nose give shape to the face.

Ponies have shorter, neater heads than horses. They often have dense coats and long, thick manes. Here, try using a fairly hard 3H pencil for the outline and lighter shadows. Use a softer HB for the darker ears, eyes, nostrils and mane.

A heavy horse

The creases in the neck are done in colored pencil.

Heavy horses like this Suffolk Punch have thicker, broader heads and blunter muzzles than the lightweight breeds. Including the whole neck in this picture increases the impression of the horse's massive size and muscle power.

The eye is in line with the ear tip.

The top of the nostril is about level with the point where the head joins the neck.

Keep the outlines light for a soft look.

Foals have leaner, less well-defined heads than adults. The blue construction lines shown above will help you position the features correctly. As foals have fluffy coats and manes, a soft drawing material, such as colored pencil, works best.

A bridled head

Make the straps curve to show how they fasten around the whole head and to give a three-dimensional look to the face.

The detailed bridle is done with a very fine brush.

Adding a bridle helps to frame the head and add character. First draw the whole head and face in detail, then add the bridle. Narrow straps look best on this horse but a wide noseband and browband would suit a heavy horse better.

The paces

Horses have four different paces, or gaits. A single moment from each of the gaits is illustrated on these pages. The pictures also show, in sequence, how color can be built up using colored pencils.

Walk

This is a smooth, gentle four-beat gait in which the horse lifts and sets down each hoof, one at a time.

Trot

In this springy, two-beat motion, opposite legs, known as diagonals, move together. To begin coloring the horse, apply a smooth layer of the base colors over the whole body.

The neck is held long and relaxed.

Mark out the positions of the eyes, nostrils, mane and mouth.

The hooves flick back as they are lifted.

Initially, make the shading very light on the tail, mane and legs.

The neck is arched.

The head is carried high, but held still.

Add a second layer of color to areas that are in shadow.

Canter

This is a bounding, three-beat movement. The horse sets down one back hoof, then a pair of diagonals together, then the last front hoof. Add reddish-brown over the horse, letting the base color show through on highlighted parts.

The head is held high and swings as the horse moves.

Use reddish-brown to show the shapes of the flexing muscles on the shoulders, legs, neck and hindquarters.

Gallop

This is the fastest and most dramatic pace, in which there is even a moment when all four hooves are off the ground at the same time.

Use black streaks to thicken the mane, then add white highlights.

The streaming mane and tail emphasize the horse's speed.

Add dark reddish-brown to the undersides, under the muscles and along the back. Put a thin layer of black on the most shadowy areas.

Go to **www.usborne-quicklinks.com** for a link to a site where you can watch some simple, animated versions of the paces.

A rearing horse

Horses are lively and can be nervous. They may rear if startled or excited. A horse rearing high on its hind legs makes a dramatic picture.

Here you can see how the watercolor horse on the opposite page was done, starting with the basic shapes shown on the right.

This foreleg is almost at right angles to the weightline.

Draw a vertical weightline through the horse's hindquarters and hocks as shown. This will help make the horse appear properly balanced.

Try to keep the pencil lines smooth.

The mane and tail are the same color as the parts of the body from which they grow.

Keeping the pencil marks quite soft, smooth off the outline and erase any lines which will not appear on the final drawing. Mark in the edges of the piebald (black and white) patches, and sketch the eyes, nostrils and mouth.

Paint a base layer of violet over the areas where the black patches will be, to give it a rich sheen. Apply a layer of pale pink to the hooves. Some dabs of pale gray in shadowy areas will start to give shape to the white parts of the coat.

Build up the darker shades but let the white paper and the violet base show through on the highlighted parts of the coat.

Pinkish-beige watercolor and gray pencil stripes give the hooves shape.

Blend the edges of the black patches with a little gray paint to show where they merge with the white patches.

Too much solid black makes a picture look flat, so only use it on the parts of the horse which are in deep shadow. Use pale blue or violet colored pencils to add highlights to the black areas.

Using contrast makes the muscles on the legs and hindquarters stand out. Apply dark lines and pale highlights to the dark patches. For the white patches, use some gray or yellowish-brown pencils to define the muscle lines.

As a finishing touch, streaks of white colored pencil prevent the tail from looking solid.

203

A bucking horse

Bucking is a sign of high spirits, although broncos, like the one below, use it to unseat their riders. Bronco means "rough" in Spanish. The picture on this page was done in colored pencils.

Cowboys ride bucking broncos in competitions called rodeos. The cowboy tries to stay on for up to ten seconds, gripping with only one hand and his knees.

Do the horse first, then the cowboy. His elbow, knee and boot tip form a straight line parallel with the line between the horse's shoulder and knee.

The flying hat gives a sense of movement.

Use a sharp, 2B pencil for fine features such as the eye and boot.

Let the paper show through where the tail catches the light.

The shadow on the ground shows how high the horse's quarters are in the air.

A few movement lines around the bronco help to convey its jolting motion.

Color the horse's coat with a pale layer of golden-yellow. Try not to let the pencil strokes show, so that this layer looks as flat as possible. Put some gray and gold streaks into the mane and tail and lightly shade the cowboy.

Slowly build up layers of richer, darker shades. Look at where the light is hitting the horse and rider, and add shadows accordingly. To achieve the lovely sheen on the horse's coat, let the golden-yellow base shine through in the lightest areas.

204

Dressage

Dressage is a popular event among horse riders. A dressage test tries to show that the horse is highly obedient, supple and balanced, and that the rider can control it easily. To do this, they have to perform various set movements. Try copying the picture on this page, starting with the basic shapes on the right.

Draw the shapes and lines of the horse first. The right foreleg and left hind leg are parallel.

The straight lines shown in green help you to find the height of the rider.

This horse and rider are performing an extended trot. The horse stays in a trotting rhythm, but stretches its legs more than usual.

The stiffness of the rider contrasts nicely with the strong movement of the horse.

The tail fluttering out adds a touch of freedom to the very formal pose.

The horse's nose forms a vertical line parallel with the rider's position.

A long, dark shadow on the ground suggests how the horse is stretched out.

Go to *www.usborne-quicklinks.com* for a link to a Web site where you'll find lots of dressage photos you can use for drawing practice.

Cross country

Cross country is a tough equestrian sport and it requires speed and stamina. The picture on this page was done using colored pencils and a little white paint for the splashes of water. Try copying it by laying some tracing paper over it and picking out the basic shapes and lines. Refine the outlines and transfer them to white paper before adding color.

The rider's body is parallel with the horse.

Do the horse first. Use bold lines to capture its powerful, surging movement.

Use flecks of white paint for the flying water drops on the coat.

A great splash of water gives a sense of the horse springing forward and up.

The water is a blend of light blue, green and purple. Let streaks of white show through to make it gleam.

206

A jumping pony

This picture is very dramatic because of the angle from which it is drawn. The strong contrast between the dark and light areas also adds to its impact. A 3H pencil was used to shade the paler areas, while the eyes, jacket and boots were done in a softer HB.

In this picture, the front hooves look bigger than the back ones. This effect, where the body proportions are altered because of the angle from which the body is seen, is called foreshortening.

Look closely at the construction lines shown on the left to see how the various parts of the pony and rider are positioned in relation to each other.

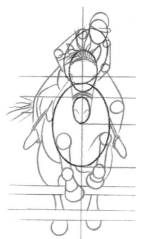

The rider's knees are level with the top of the muzzle.

Leave the rear hooves with hardly any shading, to make them look farther back.

The three main ovals in the pony's body overlap and much of the body is hidden, because the pony is coming toward you.

Leave plenty of white space under the fence to make it look as if the pony is high in the air.

*Go to **www.usborne-quicklinks.com** for a link to a Web site where you can learn more about foreshortening.*

Show jumping

Show jumping is a tough test of a horse's fitness and suppleness.

This picture uses gouache for a powerful, dynamic effect. It is drawn from low down, so that the viewer is looking up at the horse. This helps increase the sense of height and make the jump look impressive.

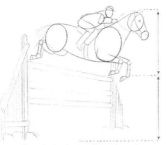

Sketch the horse first, then the rider. Put the jump in last. In the sketch above, the distance from the ears to the fetlocks is about the same as between the fetlocks and the base of the jump.

Working over the rough shapes, do an accurate pencil sketch of the horse, the rider and the jump. Erase the lines you don't need. Try to keep the outline looking smooth.

Paint a gray base coat, as shown on the hindquarters above, over the whole horse. Paint flat base coats over the jump and rider. Start to add paler highlights and darker shadows to the horse to give it form, as shown on the neck.

Drawing details

Make the hoof mid-brownish gray. Shade the front and back, and along the top.

Soft dark and light stripes, very close together, show the bony hoof texture.

Draw the eye shape and sketch the lid above it. Make the eye black and the lid dark gray.

The eye is darkest around the edges and has a white highlight. Add a line around the eyelid.

Although the horse is black, only the darkest parts are actually painted solid black. Most of the coat is painted in shades of gray, to show the glossy highlights. The strongest highlights, such as those on the hindquarters, are almost white.

The eye has a dot of white in it to make it look shiny.

By showing no background you can ensure that the horse and rider are the focus of attention.

A highlight on the closest knee makes it stand out from the one behind, as well as making it look glossy.

Brushstrokes going in the direction of the growth of the coat help to make it look sleek and well-groomed.

209

Cartoon horses

Horses work well as cartoons because of their big, expressive heads, gangly, long legs, and shaggy manes and tails. Here are some suggestions for ways to use these features to create comic effects. Opposite you can see how various horse colors and markings can add character to your cartoons and make a picture funny.

A carthorse

A smooth, bold outline gives the drawing more impact.

Apply a flat, gold base.

Exaggerating the mouth into a grin adds humour.

The "feathers" on the horse's legs can be drawn like flared pants-legs.

With a soft pencil, such as a 2B, sketch the basic shapes as shown above. Exaggerating the size of the head and features like the eyes and mouth adds a humorous touch.

When the outlines are right, go over them with a fine, black, waterproof felt-tip pen. Finally, the coat color, shading and details should be added using colored inks or felt-tip pens for a bright, solid effect.

Use long, wavy, black lines for the tail and feathers.

Shadows can be added in ink or felt-tip pen when the base is dry.

A few extra hairs around the muzzle make it look shaggy.

Highlights should be done last, in white ink or colored pencil.

Comical coat colors

Appaloosa

Skewbald

White blaze

Different coat colors and markings create different impressions in your cartoons. Spotted Appaloosa horses look

clown-like with their "rash" of irregular dark spots on a white face. The broad brown and white patches of the skewbald

make a funny, quirky pattern, while a wide white blaze on a colored head adds a lot of goofy character.

An old ranch horse

A missing tooth and some stray whiskers give a worn, comical look.

The back is slightly pointed where the old spine has weakened.

See if you can figure out the basic shapes of this bony old horse for yourself. The body shapes on the opposite page may help. To get the right sense of character, look closely at all the details, for example, the lumpy knees, the movement lines and the crossed eyes as the horse focuses on the carrot.

Large hooves on spindly legs give a plodding effect.

A few movement lines suggest the horse is unsteady on its feet.

211

Different breeds

Each breed of horse or pony has a unique set of features. Drawing them is really good practice because you have to pay very close attention to get a good likeness. Here are pictures of four distinct breeds, showing their most notable features.

Arab

This is one of the most ancient, pure and beautiful of all breeds. It is a fairly small but compact, strong horse, full of grace and stamina. These qualities and its gentle nature make it very popular as both a show and riding horse.

Breton

This is a French heavy horse, used mainly for farm work. It has a sturdy, thickset build, with different proportions than the lightweight breeds. The legs are much shorter than usual (try comparing them with the horse on pages 196-197). The head is squarish and set on a massive, short neck.

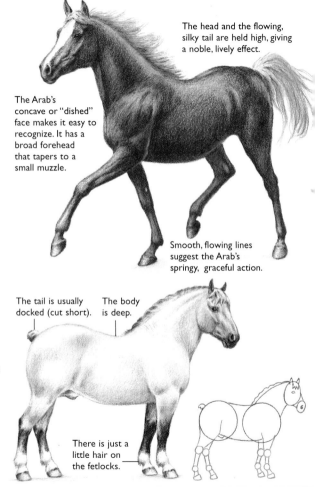

The head and the flowing, silky tail are held high, giving a noble, lively effect.

The Arab's concave or "dished" face makes it easy to recognize. It has a broad forehead that tapers to a small muzzle.

Smooth, flowing lines suggest the Arab's springy, graceful action.

The tail is usually docked (cut short).

The body is deep.

There is just a little hair on the fetlocks.

Go to **www.usborne-quicklinks.com** *for a link to a Web site where you will find pictures and information on different horse breeds of the world.*

Shetland pony

The Shetland is one of the smallest of the pony breeds, but is extremely strong and tough for its size. To capture the dense, fluffy look of its winter coat, do lots of short strokes very close together, or use colored pencils on a rough-surfaced paper.

The ears are tiny and neat.

The body is compact and set on very short legs.

Long, wavy strokes give the mane and tail their full, shaggy look.

American Saddlebred

This spectacular horse is especially well known for its action. As well as the usual paces, it can be trained to do two extra gaits, including the rack. This is a flashy, exciting pace in which the horse moves each foot individually and in an even rhythm, but very fast. The Saddlebred carries its head and tail very high, giving it a spirited, elegant look which is unmistakable.

The head is carried high on a long, curving neck.

The foal's head is much smaller than the adult's.

The tail sits high and gives a showy look.

The tail is short and fluffy.

The foal's legs are very long and slender in relation to its body.

The hooves are grown unusually long to draw attention to the horse's movement.

2 13

Pegasus

The light green construction lines help get the angle of the wing right.

The fine, detailed shading along each feather and between the layers adds weight to the wing. A 3H pencil is best for this, as it gives a soft effect without smudging.

For dark parts such as the nostril, use an HB pencil.

This fabulous winged horse is a character from Greek mythology. It was tamed by Bellerophon, a warrior, who used the horse to help him conquer a monster called the Chimera. Pegasus later became the horse of Zeus, the father of the gods, and was used to carry thunderbolts.

In this picture, the bold, curving outline echoes the strong, soaring movement. Leave white highlights as shown and use plenty of dense, detailed shading to bring out the shape of the horse.

*Go to **www.usborne-quicklinks.com** for a link to a Web site where you can read an animated storybook of the Bellerophon myth.*

Internet links

For links to more Web sites about horses and how to draw them, go to the Usborne Quicklinks Web site at **www.usborne-quicklinks.com** and click on the number of the Web site you want to visit.

Web site 1 Here you'll find lots of tips and help on drawing horses from a professional equestrian artist called Claudia Coleman. There are three lessons in total, covering proportions, perspective and shading.

Web site 2 You can view a selection of Claudia Coleman's own equestrian paintings at this site.

Web site 3 If you're crazy about horses, then this is the site for you. It's filled with interactive games, quizzes and word searches that will help you learn more about horses and how to care for them. There are also lots of pictures to download, print out and color.

Web site 4 Here you can view a gallery of beautiful horse paintings and drawings by a Canadian artist. Click on **originals** to see the first page of pictures, then select **More**, at the bottom of the page, to view the rest of the gallery. You can see an enlargement by clicking on each individual picture.

Web site 5 This one's definitely just for fun. Create a whole horse-themed desktop by downloading the free desktop package and screensavers. There are also some fun jokes and heart-warming horse tales to read.

Web site 6 Here you'll find a selection of really good horse pictures to copy. Click on a title from the list and it will be displayed on the screen. You can then draw directly from the screen.

Web site 7 Here, you can explore a cave in the south west of France which contains prehistoric paintings of horses and other animals. To go on a virtual tour of the cave, click on **discover** followed by **virtual visit**. You can use the clickable map to explore the cave.

Web site 8 At this site you can see an online exhibition about how horses have featured in sport, both past and present. Click on a title to find out more and see an accompanying painting.

Web site 9 Horses have always been one of people's best friends in the animal world. At this site, you can read about the history and evolution of horses, and how they have helped humans through the ages.

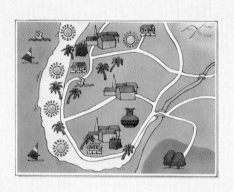

HOW TO DRAW
MAPS

Pam Beasant and Alastair Smith

Edited by Lisa Miles and Judy Tatchell
Designed by Nigel Reece and Fiona Brown
Illustrated by Peter Dennis, Colin King,
Guy Smith and Cathy Simpson
Additional designs by Iain Ashman

Consultants: Rosemary Duncan and Craig Asquith

CONTENTS

218 Drawing maps
220 A basic map
224 Showing map details
226 Old maps
228 Modern cartography
229 New maps
230 World maps
232 Maps for your wall
234 Diagram and pattern maps
236 A fantasy map
238 Floor plans
239 Internet links

Drawing maps

Maps and charts are visual ways of showing complicated information clearly. As well as having practical purposes, such as showing a route or a set of facts, maps and charts can also make vivid, attractive pictures or colorful posters for your walls.

About maps

Maps show the outline of an area and its features. Some maps show routes and landmarks. Others show facts, such as how many people live in that area. Below are some aspects of map drawing which are explained later in this section.

Scale

You can make a map of an area almost any size you like. This technique is called drawing to scale. This is a medium-scale map.

Symbols

Maps use symbols to show real features. This saves space and makes them easy to read. The meaning of each symbol is clear.

Decoration

Maps can be decorated with intricate patterns, borders and symbolic pictures to add brightness and character.

Color

Different colors and types of shading can be used to show facts, such as the height of the land, or the depth of the sea.

Professional map production

Professional mapmakers, called cartographers, use great skill and sophisticated computer equipment to make their maps.

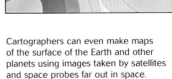

Cartographers can even make maps of the surface of the Earth and other planets using images taken by satellites and space probes far out in space.

About charts

Charts show information visually in the form of a diagram, so that it can be understood at a glance. You can choose different types of chart to show your information.

For example, both the pie chart and the bar chart below show the number and type of pets owned by a group of people. You can decorate your charts to reflect what they show.

On a pie chart, different amounts are represented by different-sized sections of a circle.

1 parrot

5 rabbits

7 fish

6 dogs

5 gerbils

3 cats

Bar charts divide information into blocks. Different amounts are shown by blocks of different heights.

NUMBER OF PEOPLE

7					
6					
5					
4					
3					
2					
1					
0| fish	cat	gerbil	dog	rabbit	parrot

TYPE OF PET

Drawing tools

You can do the projects in this section using equipment that is easily available in most art supply stores. Some useful items are shown here.

You need plain paper for drawing or thicker art paper for painting.

Soft-leaded pencils are good for sketching and shading. Hard-leaded pencils are good for fine lines and detail.

Felt-tip pens and colored pencils can be used for most of the maps and charts in this section.

Watercolor paints are useful for large areas of color and an even finish.

A ruler, a pair of compasses and a flexible curve ruler will help you draw accurate angles and curves.

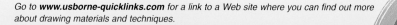

*Go to **www.usborne-quicklinks.com** for a link to a Web site where you can find out more about drawing materials and techniques.*

A basic map

A map showing the area around your home is one of the simplest to draw. As well as main roads, it can include places such as churches and parks.

Over the next four pages you can find out how to plan a route between your house and a nearby place, such as a friend's house.

Stage 1: rough sketch

Start by drawing a small square (your home) in one corner of a sheet of paper. Make a rough sketch from memory of all the roads between your house and your friend's house. Draw the map so that it fills the paper. When all the roads are in place, draw your friend's house.

Stage 2: measuring the roads

Measure the route by walking along it and counting the number of paces. Note the paces between each junction on your rough map. Plot on the map any landmarks that you see. Sketch any streets that you go past. Note the names of streets that you do not know.

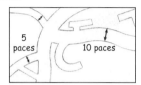

Be careful and do not measure while crossing roads. Use standard widths such as five paces for a narrow road and ten for a wider one. Make rough sketches of the angles at which streets meet. You do not need to draw them accurately at this stage.

Map facts: scale

A map scale tells how much real distance is represented by a distance shown on the map. Once real distances have been measured, a scale is chosen so that the map can be drawn accurately and fitted on the sheet of paper to be used.

Country maps are often small-scale. 1in represents a long distance, such as 50miles.

A road map is medium-scale. 1in stands for less distance than on a small-scale map, such as 1mile.

Maps you can draw from the instructions on these pages are large-scale. 1in stands for a short distance, say 50 paces.

Stage 3: choosing a scale

To choose your scale, count the number of paces down the longest road you measured. As an example, if the longest street is 500 paces, a good scale might be 1in = 50 paces. On the map, the street would be 10in long.

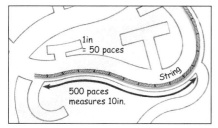

Draw the scaled measurement of the street on some paper and check it to see if you think that your whole map will fit. If the road is curved, you could measure it using a piece of string, marked off in centimetres or half inches.

Street lengths
Long Avenue - 150 paces = 3in
Main Road - 250 paces = 5in
High Street - 800 paces = 16in
Bridge Street - 25 paces = ½in

Once you have decided on your scale, convert all your measurements, so that you know how long the roads will need to be. (If you have an awkward number of paces, round them up or down to the nearest tenth.)

Stage 4: north and south

Most maps are drawn so that north is at the top and south is at the bottom. North is usually drawn on a map as an arrow with the letter N at the top.

To find north on your map, stand outside your home and line up the road on your map with the direction of the real road.

Using a compass, find the direction of north and mark it on your map. You can buy a compass from a sporting goods store.

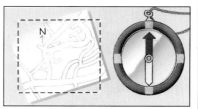

When you draw your map out neatly, north should be at the top. The red lines show how the finished map will be positioned.

Go to www.usborne-quicklinks.com for a link to a Web site where you can compare different kinds of maps of the same place.

Stage 5: symbols

Most maps use symbols to represent details. This makes them clearer and easier to draw. When you draw your map, decide which symbols you will use to show landmarks. Write a list of all the things you need to show and draw the symbol you will use beside each item. Make each symbol very clear and simple. In a corner of your map, show all your symbols in a box and write the meanings clearly beside each symbol. This is called a key. The key on the map opposite is in the top left corner.

Bakery

Fast food

Large tree

Library

Swimming pool

Cinema

Ice rink

Video store

Spooky house

Bank

Post office

Pond

Stage 6: drawing the map

1. Using your rough map as a guide, start plotting the roads on tracing paper, using pencil. Begin with a large crossroads, or a similar prominent feature. Add the other major roads.

2. Mark in the side roads (use string to measure them if they are curved). Make sure that the roads fit together properly.

3. Now position the two houses and landmarks. Use the symbols you have chosen.

4. Draw a box for the key and the map title (see title boxes on page 223).

5. Turn the tracing paper over. On the back of the paper, draw over the lines of the map with a pencil.

6. Lay the paper right side up over fresh paper. Go over the lines to transfer them to the fresh paper. Then ink in the lines and color the map.

7. Write the scale near the edge of the map. (See page 225 for ways to write scales.)

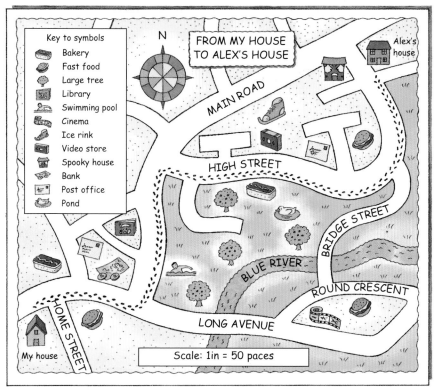

Borders

This map has been drawn with a white border around it. A map border is called a neatline. Alternatively, you could draw your map up to the edge of the paper.

Title boxes

If you like, you can give your map a title and write it in a title box. Decorated title boxes are called cartouches. You can find out more on page 227.

Drawing in the route

Your preferred route can be shown in several ways. Footprints show that you can walk there. You could use arrows or a colored line instead.

223

Showing map details

Maps of the same area can look different depending on the way they are drawn. For example, information about climate or what types of plants grow in a certain area can be shown as different shades or with symbols. The examples of map details that appear on these pages show some of the techniques you can use on all your map projects.

Buildings

On medium-scale maps, simple silhouettes can show the positions of important buildings, such as churches.

Buildings are plotted in more detail on larger-scale maps. Important buildings are drawn as if you are looking down on them.

Forests

You can use small tree symbols to represent forests. The closer together the trees are, the denser the forest is.

Graded shades of green using colored pencil can also show the density of trees.

Showing height

Maps that show land height are called relief maps. Ways of showing height, such as contours, may also show steepness. Lines drawn up and down a hill, called hachures, get thicker as the ground gets steeper.

Steep slope

Top of hill

Gentle slope

Steep slope

Gentle slope

A technique called stippling uses small dots. They are closer together as the hill gets steeper.

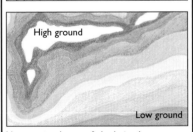

High ground

Low ground

You can use layers of shade to show different heights. Usually, the lowest ground is shown in green and the highest is in white.

*Go to **www.usborne-quicklinks.com** for a link to a Web site where you can get more information and play a game about how to read contour maps.*

Coastlines

Coastlines can have hachures added to them to indicate high cliffs. Shadows can give a similar effect.

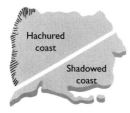

Sea

The sea can be shown in many ways, such as small blue dots, or wavy blue lines. You could show different depths of water by using different shades of blue.

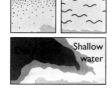

Deserts

You could draw small hills on a yellow background to show dunes in a desert. A symbol, such as a camel or a cactus, will add to the effect.

Ice and snow

You could use white paint, chalk or white pencil to show areas of ice and snow. Cover the whole area, or draw large white snowflake symbols to represent snow.

The igloo shows an area that is always under snow.

How to read contours

Contours connect land of the same height. They are drawn on maps to show where hills are and how steep they are. Contours can also be used to show the depth of water.

If the contours are close together, the hill is steep.

If the contours are far apart, the hill slopes gently.

Writing a scale

There are three main ways of writing scales on maps.

1. Linear scale. Each section represents the same distance. Routes can easily be measured using this method shown below.

0 miles	¾	1½	
0 km	1	2	3

2. Representative fraction. The first figure is a distance on the map. The second is the real distance it represents. Both figures use the same units.

3. Written scale. This scale is simply written out.

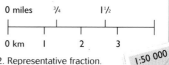

Maps that show natural features, such as forests or hills, are called physical maps.

Old maps

Before printing was invented, maps had to be drawn by hand and painted individually. They were very rare and often considered to be works of art in themselves. These pages show some examples of ancient maps and explain how to decorate your own maps so that they look as though they were drawn hundreds of years ago.

Map facts: oldest maps

The oldest surviving maps were made around 500BC by the Babylonians from the Middle East. They carved the maps on clay slabs called tablets.

Ptolemy's world map

The Greek scholar, Claudius Ptolemy, produced maps of the world in the second century AD. He based his drawings on mathematical calculations, and information provided by sailors and explorers. According to Ptolemy's findings, Europe, Africa and Asia were the only continents in the world. He did not know that America, Australia and Antarctica existed. The map on the left was based on Ptolemy's information. The faces around the edge of the map represent the winds.

New discoveries

As Europeans discovered new parts of the world, they included them on their maps. This map was made in the late 17th century. It shows that America and Australia had been discovered. Parts of the world that had not been explored by Europeans at that time were left blank.

This map would have belonged to someone very important. It is highly decorated with pictures representing the elements earth, air, fire and water. The men in the four corners are famous mapmakers and kings.

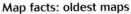

Town map

This map of New York was drawn in 1664, when the city was much smaller than it is today. The city ends at a wall, which was built to protect the citizens from attack. Wall Street now stands on the site of this wall.

The map shows drawings of things like buildings and ships. The effect is a cross between a map and a drawing of the sights you would have seen in New York at that time. The title box of the map is very grand, to reflect the importance of New York. This type of title box is called a cartouche. You can see more cartouches below.

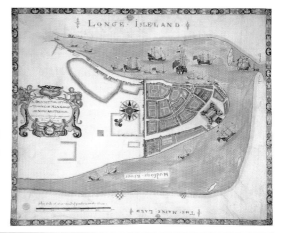

Cartouches

Cartouches are decorated panels containing the title of a map or a key to its symbols. They were first drawn on Italian maps in the 15th century. They often showed flowers, fruit or birds, as well as fancy scrolls and swirls. Sometimes they showed things associated with the map. Navigation maps, for instance, might have shown ships and anchors.

You can draw cartouches to decorate your own maps. You could make up a simple pattern, or draw pictures associated with the map. You could draw windsurfers on a map of a tourist resort, for example.

Treasure map cartouche

This cartouche would suit a Pirate's treasure map. It contains drawings of the treasure as well as some of the things you might encounter on a treasure-hunting expedition.

Pirate's Treasure Map

On pages 236–237 you can find out how to draw a mysterious fantasy map. You can take inspiration from the examples on these pages to include a cartouche and other decorative details on your version.

Modern cartography

Today, cartographers have a range of accurate instruments which they use to record map details. Map production relies on very advanced equipment and technology. However, the cartographers' skill in gathering and analyzing information and putting the map together is still a very important part of the process.

This aerial photograph shows details of a city.

The map was drawn using the aerial photograph as a guide.

Gathering information

Before drawing a map, cartographers need to know all the information which is relevant to their map. They research the area thoroughly and study any existing base maps of it.

Surveyors visit the area to note details about what is on the ground. For a town map, buildings are plotted and angles of streets are measured. For a relief map, heights of hills are measured.

Aerial photographs (photographs taken from high above, looking down) are valuable to cartographers. They provide a bird's-eye view of the land and help match up the position of landmarks.

Modern technology

Modern technology, such as satellite imagery and radar, helps cartographers gather information without actually going to a place and measuring it. This technique is called remote sensing. Cartographers use computers to store and produce digital maps from the information that they collect.

Satellites take pictures of the Earth's atmosphere and its surface. Cartographers use these like aerial photographs, to help them produce weather maps and relief maps.

The satellite photograph on the left is of Sacramento, CA. It shows clear details, such as built-up areas, rivers and mountains.

Go to **www.usborne-quicklinks.com** for a link to a Web site where you can see lots of different satellite images of the Earth.

New maps

The range of equipment available to cartographers today means that they can even make maps of things that cannot be seen by the naked eye, such as information about weather or climate changes. The use of satellites, telescopes and space probes has also enabled maps to be made of far-off galaxies.

Satellite images

Satellites can be used to plot things like landforms and weather conditions. This sort of information is crucial to weather forecasters. The satellite image below shows a storm about to hit the East coast of America. The curled cloud is a hurricane.

Star maps

Some satellites carry telescopes which look at distant stars. The results are used to make accurate star maps. In space, telescopes are more powerful than on Earth because they are beyond the haze of Earth's atmosphere.

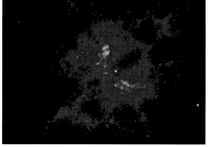

The white dot in the middle of the red gas cloud is a star.

Space maps

Here, lots of flat, digital images of Mars, taken by a space probe, have been joined together and wrapped around a sphere to produce this computer-generated picture.

World maps

All world maps are distorted, because it is impossible to show all of the Earth's curve accurately on a flat map. Differently distorted views of the world, called projections, can be created. The two projections below were created by the same cartographer over a hundred years ago.

Equal area projection

In this projection, the sizes of areas of land are correct in relation to each other. However, the shape of most of the land is distorted.

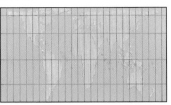

Accurate shape projection

This projection is useful for giving an idea of the shapes of areas of land. It is not accurate for showing the relative sizes of areas of land.

Map facts: latitude and longitude

A grid of numbered lines is drawn on world maps. This divides the world into imaginary sections to help people to find places on the map. Latitude lines run horizontally and longitude lines run vertically.

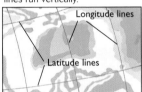

Longitude lines

Latitude lines

The maps on the left are marked with latitude and longitude lines. The line positions are different on each map because of the different projections.

A cut up globe

The most accurate way to show the world on flat paper is to show it as strips of a peeled globe. A map of this kind is very tricky to read, though, because gaps are left between parts of the world. The picture on the right shows curved strips peeled from a globe and laid out flat, to make a map of the world.

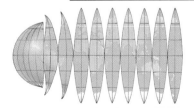

*Go to **www.usborne-quicklinks.com** for a link to a Web site with basic outline maps of countries or regions for you to print and fill in with your own details.*

Wildlife map of the world

This map shows wildlife from some regions of the world. You could draw a version of it, showing any animals you choose. You can find pictures of animals in magazines, then cut them out and stick them on the map. If you want to draw the animals yourself, you can follow the steps below. You may want to make a bigger map so that you can display it on your wall. On page 232 you can see how to enlarge your wildlife map and there are ideas for other maps you can make.

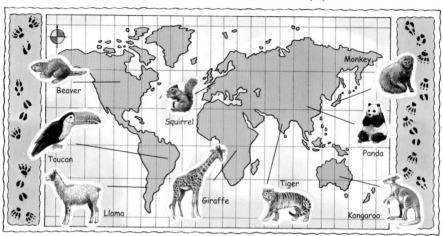

Beaver

Squirrel

Monkey

Toucan

Panda

Llama

Giraffe

Tiger

Kangaroo

Animal shapes

Animals can be complicated, but fun to draw. You can follow these steps to make your animal drawings easier. Adding animal pictures to your wildlife map will make it much more attractive. You can find out more about drawing animals on pages 122-143.

Use a pencil to draw the basic shapes that make up each animal. You can erase these lines later.

Fill in the shapes and make your animals look realistic by coloring in the details such as eyes, noses, fur and feet.

Maps for your wall

You can make large versions of maps, such as the ones in this section, to put on your wall. By decorating them in different ways you can use your wall maps to show a variety of information. These pages show you how to enlarge your maps to poster size and give you ideas on how to decorate them.

Enlarging a map

 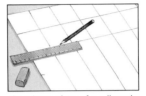 

To draw a map large enough to go on your wall, choose the map you want to use in an atlas or book. If it does not have lines of latitude and longitude on it, place a piece of tracing paper over the map to draw a grid.

On a large piece of cardboard, draw an enlarged grid in pencil with the same number of squares as the original. To make the map twice the size, space the lines on the grid twice as far apart.

Copy the map square by square onto the cardboard. Then erase the grid. Finally, decorate the map. Use bright colors so that you can see the map clearly from a distance when it is on the wall.

Weather map

You could make weather symbols to tack onto your map, like those shown below. Reposition the symbols every day, according to the weather forecasts.

Rain

Thunderstorms

Sun

Clouds

Sunny intervals

Snow

Temperature

Wind speed

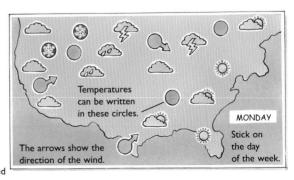

Temperatures can be written in these circles.

The arrows show the direction of the wind.

MONDAY

Stick on the day of the week.

World events map

On an outline map of the world, you could highlight any areas where important events happen. Use symbols like the ones below to show events. Color the countries where events happen.

War

International conference

Election

Hurricane

Volcano

Sports event

Earthquake

Famine

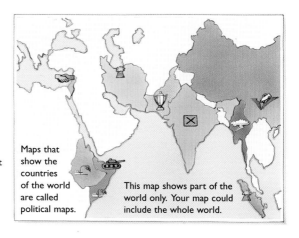

Maps that show the countries of the world are called political maps.

This map shows part of the world only. Your map could include the whole world.

Tourist map

You could draw a map of an area that you visited on your travels. Using simple symbols, indicate the places that you visited and the things that you did during your stay.

Swimming

Windsurfing

Sunbathing

Forest trail

Town

Museum

Restaurant

Shops

233

Diagram and pattern maps

Maps do not have to represent every detail of an area. They can be made to look like diagrams. This is useful for route maps, where a complicated network can be simplified to make it easier to read, as shown on this page. On the opposite page are maps drawn in particular styles. Such maps are often used in advertisements because they are eye-catching.

Making a route map

Most transportation systems have route maps. The routes are simplified and color-coded so that people can follow them easily. The lines between stops do not represent real distances to scale.

Follow the steps on this page to make a clear route map of your imaginary transportation system for your area.

You could think up ways to draw different types of transportation on your map. Use straight lines for bus routes and broken lines for train routes, for instance.

Drawing the map

Here, two routes share a road.

1. Trace your network from a map of your area. Use a different color for each route, to make them stand out from each other.

2. Mark where you want stops to be on each route. You could mark stops near a variety of places, such as stores or a school.

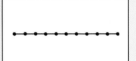

3. Redraw the simplest route, making its shape more diagrammatic and regular. Make spaces equal between each stop.

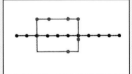

4. Redraw a second route, starting with the stops that it shares with the simplest route. Space the other stops evenly.

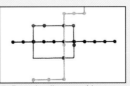

5. Draw in all routes. You may need to draw several versions, adjusting the positions of the stops, until it all fits together.

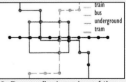

train
bus
underground
tram

6. Draw a final version of the map. Make the route map clear and colorful. Draw a key to the routes at the side.

Grid map

To draw a stylized, angular map like this, follow these stages.

1. Trace the outline of an area from a base map, using pencil.

2. Lay your tracing over a piece of graph paper. Using a fine pen, redraw the map following the graph lines that are closest to the map outline.

3. Erase the pencil lines made by your tracing of the base map. Finally, color the grid map, using bright felt-tip pens.

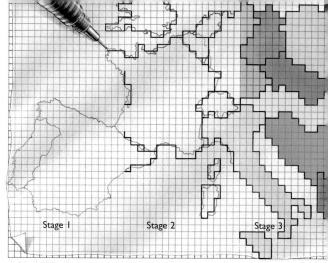

Stage 1   Stage 2   Stage 3

Circuit diagram map

An electric company might use a map like this in an advertisement. First draw a simplified pencil outline of the area you want to show.

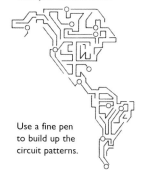

Use a fine pen to build up the circuit patterns.

Simplified shape map

The outlines of countries or continents can be made into striking shapes by simplifying the shapes of borders into a series of straight lines.

A shadow makes the shape look 3D.

Scary map

Adapt the basic shape of a country to draw a scary map like this one. Look for parts of a coastline that could become fierce faces.

235

A fantasy map

It can be fun to invent a fantasy map full of mythical creatures such as trolls, and hazards such as deadly marshes. Coded place names give the map an element of mystery. You could use this map as inspiration for your own maps or as the basis for a game. You could even draw a map based on an existing fantasy story.

Lush-looking trees show an enchanted forest.

Map details

Try to include details which add to the overall mystery of the map. You could start by making the paper look old, by crumpling it and painting it with watery tea.

Town and village buildings can be sketchy and small. This gives them an old, rickety look.

Using colors

Use colors to help convey whether an area is safe or not. For example, use warm, light shades to indicate friendly areas. Cold, murky shades are good for showing hostile areas.

Thin, wavy lines indicate the coastline.

A few dashes and clumps of grass can indicate a deadly marsh.

N

Coded alphabet

Each rune-like letter below corresponds to a letter of the alphabet. Try to decipher the place names on the map.

This compass symbol shows old weapons because the map shows a battlefield.

```
A B C D E F G H I J K L M N O P Q R S T U V W X Y Z
```

236

Important buildings are drawn in more detail than other buildings.

Mountains can be shown as a series of overlapping points. Shadows on their sides make them look 3D.

Gnarled-looking trees show a grim, haunted forest.

The scale does not need to be accurate, because fantasy stories rarely give precise distances.

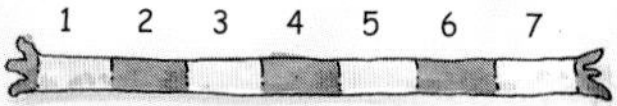

Drawing the details

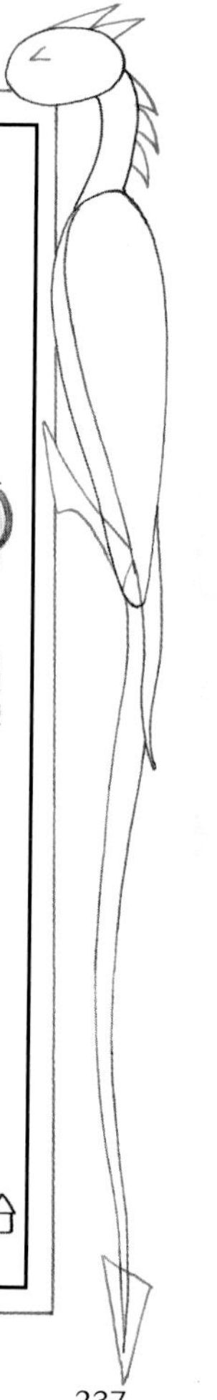

Draw creatures such as dragons using simple shapes for the body and head, before adding details. Start with the red lines, then do the blue, then the green. The border dragon can be drawn in a similar way.

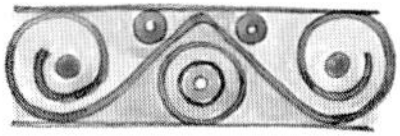

Sketch a border design in pencil, then draw over the lines in pen. Gold or silver ink can make a map look precious. Draw the lines freehand so that they are slightly wobbly. This makes a map look old.

The castles are made up of a few basic shapes. Draw the red lines first, then the blue, then the green. The shapes can be rearranged to make different kinds of large buildings, such as haunted houses.

For towns and villages, draw lots of simple shapes. Start with those at the front. Add more shapes of buildings behind them. This gives the impression of distance. A tall triangle for a church spire can be effective.

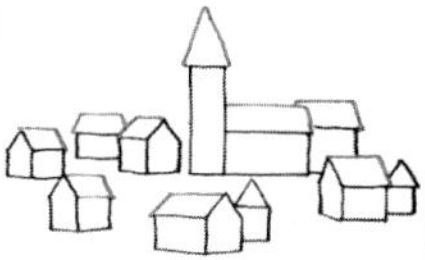

Floor plans

You can apply your mapdrawing skills to any place. A map that shows the layout of a building is called a floor plan.

Fantasy castle game

You can invent board games based on any map. This game is based on a floor plan of a fantasy castle. You can draw your own plan or trace this one and enlarge it. Make counters for each player, with different colors or designs on them.

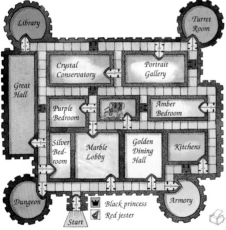

Each player starts at the main door and throws a die to move their counter around the castle, a square at a time. If you land on a yellow door, you can enter the room. If you land on a red trap door, you can enter any room. Once you have visited every room in the house, go to the treasure chest in the middle of the castle. The first player to reach the treasure is the winner.

Thematic maps

Maps that show information which compares numbers and amounts of things are called thematic maps. You could draw a thematic map of your home to compare the amount of time you spend in each room over 24 hours.

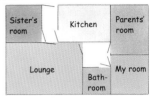

First draw a floor plan of your home as it really looks. You don't need to be completely accurate, since the sizes will be distorted later.

ROOM	TIME	SQUARES
My room	9hrs	36
Parents' room	0hrs	-
Kitchen	45mins	3
Bathroom	1hr	4
Lounge	3hrs	12
Sister's room	1hr 30mins	6
Out of house	8hrs 45mins	-

Take a note of how long you spend in each room. Using one square for every 15 minutes spent, calculate how many squares represent each room.

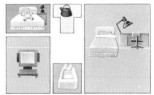

Draw the finished plan on graph paper. The distorted plan reflects the time spent in each room. Symbols show what the room is used for.

Internet links

For links to more Web sites about maps and how to draw them, go to the Usborne Quicklinks Web site at **www.usborne-quicklinks.com** and click on the number of the Web site you want to visit.

Web site 1 At the National Geographic Web site you can look at maps of anywhere in the world just by typing in the name of the region you want to see. There are also links to other National Geographic pages. Click on **Web site 2** to see star maps made from photographs taken from the Hubble Telescope. Click on **Web site 3 to** see a picture map of London.

Web site 4 This Web site is packed with information about maps of every kind. You can also pick up excellent mapmaking and map-reading skills.

Web site 5 At this Web site you can see flags for every country in the world. Just click on the map of the world to see the flags for each continent.

Web site 6 Go to this Web site to learn about latitude and find out about the tools used by fifteenth century navigators. Click **Latitude** or **Longitude** to find out more.

Web site 7 If you want to include facts about the countries on your maps, this site will provide you with the information you need about population, climate, currency, languages and lots more. You will also find links to physical and political maps that you can print out.

Web site 8 This gallery of children's maps of their communities may give you some ideas for projects of your own.

Web site 9 On this Web site, you can create different kinds of graphs to print out. Just enter your information and choose your color scheme and the style of chart you prefer.

Web site 10 Take a look at some "green" maps of environmental issues made by children around the world. To find out how to draw your own, click on **Activity Guide**.

Web site 11 If you are feeling really creative, you can follow these instructions to build your own paper globe.

Web site 12 This Web site gives a detailed, history of maps and mapmaking with lots of great photographs and pictures.

HOW TO DRAW
BUILDINGS

Pam Beasant

Designed by Iain Ashman
Edited by Judy Tatchell
Illustrated by Iain Ashman, Isobel Gardner,
Chris Lyon and Chris Smedley

Consultant: Iain Ashman
Consultant architect: Peter Reed

CONTENTS

242 Drawing buildings
244 Looking at buildings
246 Castles
248 Fantasy buildings
250 Haunted house
252 Ancient buildings
254 Skyscrapers

256 Airport
257 Train station
258 Special effects
260 Drawing and using plans
262 Tips and materials
263 Internet links

Drawing buildings

There are all sorts of exciting buildings for you to draw in this section, ranging from a cathedral to a haunted house. Clear, step-by-step instructions show you how to build up your pictures in stages.

Basic drawing and coloring skills and styles are introduced with many professional hints and techniques.

For instance, you can find out about perspective on page 247 and composition on page 256. Throughout the section there are tips on how to add convincing details such as shadows and highlights.

On pages 260–261, you can learn the basics of technical drawing and how to plan, draw and build your own model house.

There is a summary of techniques and drawing materials (such as pencils and paints) on page 262, to help you choose your equipment.

Drawing styles

The drawings in this section are done in various styles. Some of the main ones are shown here.

Pen and ink ▶

Ink color washes (see below) are added over line drawings to create shadows, highlights and graded areas of color.

Try this pen and ink haunted house on page 250.

Once you build up confidence, you can have fun experimenting with any style you choose.

◀ ### Line drawings

Line drawings are done with pen or pencil. You use lines or dots to give the impression of shadow. You can see examples of line drawings on pages 244–245 and 250–251.

Washes

A wash is a thin coat of watery paint or ink. You can add more layers for areas of stronger color or shadow. You can also mix and blend different colored washes on the same drawing.

*Go to **www.usborne-quicklinks.com** for a link to a Web site where you will see pictures of the architectural wonders of the ancient and modern world.*

Comic book style

Comic book style uses bold, black lines and deep colors. It is dramatic and can have a lot of movement.

"Impressionism" ▶

A looser style, giving an atmospheric impression of a scene, is achieved by blending soft lines and colors. Find out more about this style on pages 258–259.

◀ Dramatic angles

Different perspectives can be used to produce striking pictures from different viewpoints. This is a good way to draw large, imposing buildings like skyscrapers.

There are skyscrapers to draw on pages 254–255.

◀ Cartoons

A cartoon style can add character and a sense of fun to a drawing. It exaggerates and changes some aspects of the subject to make it funny.

There is a cartoon castle to draw on page 248.

The first layer of a wash should be very weak and watery. Then add more paint to the wash mixture to make it a darker shade. Apply each further layer when the last is dry. In this way you can gradually build up contrasting areas of light and dark.

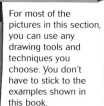

For most of the pictures in this section, you can use any drawing tools and techniques you choose. You don't have to stick to the examples shown in this book.

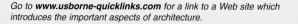

Looking at buildings

It is a good idea to carry a small sketchbook with you when you go out for a walk. You can make quick sketches of any interesting buildings or details that you see. You can use these sketches later to invent your own drawings of buildings. You could use photographs instead, although sketching helps you to see how buildings are put together.

Windows and doors

Try sketching a variety of windows and doors on one page. This is a good way to compare and contrast details and to experiment with sketching.

Fit as many details as you can onto one page.

Sketching buildings

Sketching real buildings is the best way to see how they fit together, and how their details vary. You could try drawing a street or a row of store-fronts.

Note how the shades are paler, the farther away the buildings are.

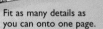

A quick, loose sketch

You can concentrate on one building in a scene. Draw just the shadowy outline of the others to frame it.

You can write small notes on your sketch about color, detail and texture.

A tight, finished sketch

Sketching a near skyline is good practice for perspective drawing.

Skylines

A skyline is often needed for background in a drawing or to give it depth. Sketching one is a good way to see the overall shape of a city.

Painting your sketches

If you take a small paintbox and a sealed water container on your sketching trip, you can paint your drawing immediately. This is a good way to practice showing realistic light and shade, and mixing lifelike colors.

 Overlap colors to emphasize shadows or darker areas.

 Dab wet paint with a tissue for a textured look.

Period styles

Every age had a different general building style. These vary around the world. There are some examples below.

Ancient Egyptian (2600-30BC)

Classical Greek (600BC)

 Islamic (700-1200)

 Romanesque (1100-1200)

 Gothic (1200-1400)

 Byzantine (1600-1700)

 Baroque (1700-1800)

 Neo-Classical (1800-1900)

 Neo-Gothic (late 1800s)

 Modern (1900-)

Go to **www.usborne-quicklinks.com** for a link to a Web site with pictures of lots of different building styles from around the world and through the ages.

Castles

Castles are huge, interesting buildings with long histories. They were built as homes by powerful people such as kings and barons. They also provided a defense against raiding enemies.

This is why their walls are so thick and high. Castles are not as hard to draw as they look. Find out below how to draw the castle shown on these two pages.

Distant mountains should be sketchy, small and not so heavily colored as the castle.

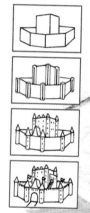

Drawing the castle

Draw the basic block shapes of the castle walls, as shown here.

Now add the shapes of the towers, erasing any unwanted lines.

Add the roofs, turrets and windows, shown here in blue.

Add the drawbridge, staircase and flags. Sketch in details such as the stonework.

The detail on the side walls can be sketchy and pale.

The drawbridge is halfway down. Draw the angles carefully.

Different kinds of castles

There are lots of different styles of castles. The main picture shows a 14th century castle.

A 12th century Norman castle

A 16th century Spanish castle

A 19th century Gothic-style German castle

A 16th century English round-walled castle

246

Paint or color only small areas of the sky.

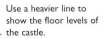

Use a heavier line to show the floor levels of the castle.

Wavy lines give the impression of a breeze.

Use thin pen lines to give the impression of roof tiles and stones. (At this distance from the castle you would not see every detail.)

Shade the areas of shadow with a heavy pencil on top of the color.

Draw short, curved lines on the water for ripples.

Cartoon castle

Cartoon castles often have a narrow base, and the towers, turrets and flags are exaggerated. Sometimes they teeter on tall, narrow rocks. There is a fairytale castle to draw on page 248.

Perspective

Drawing things "in perspective" means drawing them the way your eyes see them. Perspective is based on the idea that things look smaller the farther away they are. Pictures in perspective look real and three-dimensional (3D), rather than flat.

When you look down a street with equal sized buildings, the ones closest look much bigger than those at the other end.

On a long street, the buildings seem to get closer together until they almost meet. This imaginary meeting point is called the "vanishing point".

There is often more than one vanishing point on the same picture. Lines that are parallel to each other appear to meet at the same vanishing point.

The vanishing points are on the horizon, an imaginary eye-level line.

If you draw something from above, then the horizon is high.

If you draw something tall from below, then the horizon is low. This is called a "worm's-eye view".

If you draw something looking straight at it, then the horizon can go through the middle.

Go to www.usborne-quicklinks.com for a link to a Web site where there is a photo gallery with hundreds of pictures of castles to draw.

247

Fantasy buildings

Fantasy buildings are fun to invent and draw. The more detail you think of, the more convincing your fantasy world will be. Strange colors, figures and trees, for instance, can add life and atmosphere to your pictures. The ideas and techniques on these pages might help start you off.

Cartoons

Cartoons are not as easy as they look, because they are not strict copies of real things. Artists can use them to make jokes or comments (in newspaper cartoons for example) or to express imaginative ideas. Many of the buildings on these two pages are cartoons.

Professional cartoonists often draw quickly, using bold, incomplete lines. Try drawing a cartoon of your own house. Sketch the main shape loosely. Do not worry about getting lines too straight or filling in exact details.

Fairytale castle

In this drawing of a fairytale castle, realistic details are either exaggerated or left out altogether. There are lots of turrets, for instance, but no stonework and no roof tiles.

The colors are unrealistic, with shades of pink and purple. This helps make the castle look magical.

Compare this drawing with the castle on the previous two pages. Try to spot the things that make this one a fairytale castle.

Alien's house

This strange house belongs to an alien from a far-off planet.

248

Fantasy ideas

This house is made out of different kinds of food. The main shape is easy to draw, but the details may take some time.

These cloud-people live in strange, fluffy cloud-houses. A huge umbrella over the top keeps the rain off.

This elves' workshop is full of machines and contraptions. You could use pale colors over a dark wash for the firelight.

If you want your space house to look impressive, use a realistic style and paint or color the picture very smoothly. Try to use muted or metallic colors.

For this picture, draw the closest buildings first. Strong shadows and highlights and strange skies will help make your picture exciting and different.

Underwater city

This mysterious underwater city has been abandoned by its inhabitants. All sorts of sea creatures live here and the buildings are overgrown with seaweed.

Draw the far buildings very faintly, as if seen through murky water.

Draw broken pillars, pieces of statues lying on their sides and crumbling stairs.

Dark streaks for seaweed will give the impression of being underwater.

249

Haunted House

An old, dark house can be made to look haunted and very creepy, and is great fun to draw. Ramshackle walls and roofs with slates missing make it look abandoned and mysterious. Oddly shaped windows, strange lights behind windows and big, dark trees all give your picture lots of spooky atmosphere.

Dramatic perspective

The perspective of this haunted house makes it look huge and terrifying. It is drawn as if you are looking from ground level, so the base is wider than the top. (See page 247 for more about perspective.)

It is a bit harder to draw a house in this perspective, but it is worth trying, as your house will look very dramatic.

Moonlight suggests witches and werewolves and casts interesting light and shadow on the house.

Graded amounts of white or black added to blue paint make shades ranging from pale to deep blue. Use these on different parts of the drawing.

Look at the details on the roof and around the doors and windows. They help add a sinister feeling.

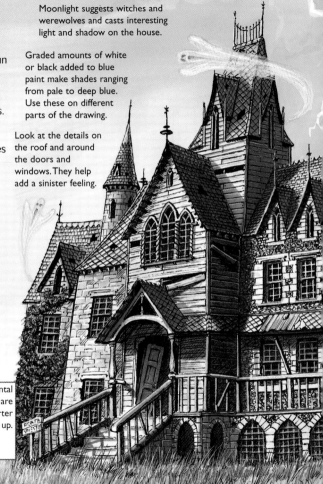

Perspective guidelines	Horizontal lines are shorter higher up.

Streaks of pale paint for lightning or to suggest flying ghosts will add atmosphere to your picture.

Large, dead trees beside the house look menacing. Make the branches thin and spiky, like fingers reaching out.

How to draw the house

First, draw the basic shape of the house. Make sure that you have left enough space for windows and doors.

Add the turrets and the jutting sections of the roof. Draw the lines straight at first. You can use them as guidelines to produce a more tumbledown look at a later stage.

Now draw the steps and the balcony at the front of the house.

Draw lines across the roof for slates. When you color the roof in, leave some black holes to show that some slates are missing.

Draw the wooden planks, leaving out a few. Draw the loose ones last, hanging down over the others.

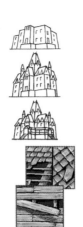

Light and shadow

The light and shadow in you picture are important as they create atmosphere. Moonlight will make part of the house light, while the rest will be in deep shadow. This suggests that things are lurking there.

Drawing shadows

Shadows always fall away from the source of light, the sun or the moon. So all the shadows should go in the same direction.

Something that is directly below the light has a short, squashed shadow.

Something standing at an angle to the light source will have a longer, more stretched shadow.

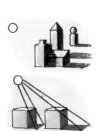

251

Ancient Buildings

Temples or churches are often the finest, most important buildings in a civilization. On these pages, you can find out how to draw four examples from around the world. The buildings date from around 1500BC to the Middle Ages.

Egyptian temple

Temples like this were built for many centuries when the Egyptians had a huge empire. The walls are covered with pictures of gods and goddesses.

1. Draw the main shape of the temple. Note that all walls slope inward.

2. Now add the raised roof, the front towers, the gateway and the flagpoles.

3. Draw the columns and the wall pictures to complete the temple.

The figures on the walls need not be too accurate, as the picture is not a close-up.

Add tiny figures at the gate to give scale.

Mayan temple

Incense was burned during sacred rituals, such as burials.

This 5th century pyramid-temple was built by the Maya people of Guatemala. Its ruins are still at the site of the Lost City of Rio Azul.

1. Draw the pyramid shape. Roughly plot then draw the cross lines and the steps.

2. Erase the pyramid peak. Draw the top building in blocks.

3. Add the stairway and sketch in the wall paintings.

Go to www.usborne-quicklinks.com for a link to a Web site where you can see some dramatic photographs of Mayan cities.

Gothic cathedral

Gothic cathedrals like this were built all over medieval Europe. The high, thin walls and turrets were richly carved.

1. Draw the blocks which make up the main shape of the building. If you draw upright lines in perspective (see page 247), a building may look as if it is leaning back. Architectural illustrators tend to draw upright lines almost vertical unless they want to create the effect of extreme height or scale (see pages 254–255).

2. Draw the roofs and turrets. Start at the front and work back.

3. Add the doors and windows. Then start to add the detail of the carved stonework.

A lighter touch gives an impression of size and distance.

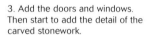

Greek temple

Temples like the one in this picture were built in Greece around the 5th century BC. The style has been copied in Europe right up to the present day.

1. Draw the main, rectangular shape. Be careful about the perspective.

2. Now draw the roof shape and mark in the tops and bottoms of columns.

3. Complete the columns and add the carved details on the front end of the building.

Skyscrapers

Skyscrapers are the tallest buildings
in the world and they can make very
dramatic pictures. They are easy
shapes to draw but the perspective
(see page 247) can be more difficult
because they are so big.

A super-hero's view

This is the way a city would look to
a super-hero swooping in to save
people from disaster. Skyscrapers
loom everywhere and the skyline in
the distance is dominated by them.

1. Start by drawing straight lines
as a perspective guide for the
skyscrapers. They should be slightly
closer together at the bottom.

2. Now draw the roofs and sides
of the buildings. Keep opposite
sides parallel. Try to picture how
the street runs below.

3. Sketch in each floor of the
skyscrapers. The lines appear
closer as you look down buildings.

4. Figure out where shadows will
fall on the buildings and shade
these areas. The shadows should be
very dark for an evening scene.

Leave some white
squares here and there
to represent lights.

The color
of buildings
should become
deeper as it
goes down.

254

A different perspective

Drawing a skyscraper from below – a worm's-eye view (see page 247) – makes it look very dramatic.

This time, the base is very wide. The sides taper up to a thin, dizzy tip, high above.

1. Tiny people show the building's height. Draw the floors closer as they go up.

2. White streaks on pale blue walls highlight the building and make it look glassy.

3. Other buildings reflected on the wall heighten the glassy look and add interest.

Drawing the skyline

Here the skyline shows the dark outline of the buildings. This is called a silhouette.

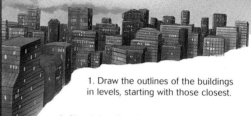

1. Draw the outlines of the buildings in levels, starting with those closest.

2. Sketch in a few details of the closest buildings, to make them less of a flat shape.

3. Color everything in dark, muted colors. Watery paint produces the best effect.

Reflections and highlights

Artists use lots of different ways to highlight areas of their drawings. Some of them are shown below.

Unpainted white areas are planned at the drawing stage.

Streaks of white pencil produce a gentle, glassy sheen.

Lines of white give a bold shine.

Black ink can show ripples and reflections.

Airport

This page shows you how to plan and draw your own exciting, aerial-view picture of an airport. It is not as hard as it looks if you build up the picture in stages.

Composition

What artists decide to show in a drawing, and from which angle, is called composition. For this airport scene, they might do several sketches from different angles to see which looks best. They could work from aerial photographs, or plans.

Plans and rough sketches

Emphasize flatness and distance by cross-hatching runways and grass in perspective, as in this picture.

Draw long, bold, "whoosh" lines behind the plane taking off.

How to draw the airport

1. Sketch the basic shapes. Drawing a grid should help you to get the perspective right.

2. Now draw the true shapes of the buildings. Add details such as the tower and windows.

3. Add the planes (see opposite) to bring the picture to life. Now add shadows and highlights.

256 Go to www.usborne-quicklinks.com for a link to a Web site where you can learn more about perspective and see how famous artists have used it in their compositions.

Train station

This drawing of a 19th century train station is difficult to do, but if you draw the perspective accurately, your picture should be convincing. A pair of compasses will help you draw the roof arches.

You can leave the roof detail fairly sketchy.

Small, sketchy figures give scale to the drawing.

There is a selection of trains you can draw below.

How to draw the station

First, draw perspective lines for the platform and the walls. They all go to a central vanishing point.

Use compasses for the roof arches. Keeping the point in the same place, make each arc wider than the last.

Draw the trains, the wall detail and the benches. Add shadows and glassy highlights to the roof.

Drawing trains and planes

These pictures might help you when drawing trains and planes.

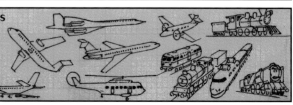

257

Special effects

Artists often use special techniques to make their drawings look funny or atmospheric. Some of them are shown on these two pages. You can use the coloring styles on any of your drawings.

You can add a face, or use windows as eyes and a door as a mouth to make buildings look like characters.
Chimneys can be drawn as hats, and add ivy for hair.

Use a bold, clear line when drawing the basic shape.

Cartoons

You can use a bold cartoon technique to make fun drawings, such as the dancing skyscrapers shown here. The buildings have to be recognizable, although the angles are distorted. The details can be sketchy.

Curved edges make buildings look flexible. Add lots of bold movement lines.

Cartoon techniques are often used to make a serious point. In this drawing a chemical factory has been made into a monster, spouting pollution from its mouth.

Coloring styles

Some artists try to capture the overall atmosphere of a scene rather than emphasize the detail. This is called impressionism. The style is quite loose, although the drawing is still accurate. You can use the techniques shown below to create an impressionist quality.

This technique uses lots of watery paint. You would need to use thick art paper for this.

Pale, washy colors run together to create a misty effect.

Bold, obvious brush strokes give a painting a sense of urgency and excitement. You can also try this with felt-tip pens or colored pencils.

You could try pastels or colored pencils for a similar effect.

There is often a great emphasis on the light and shadow of a scene.

Floodlit building

This floodlit building was painted in white and shades of gray over a dark wash.

You could use a white pencil on black paper instead. After shading, details are added in pen.

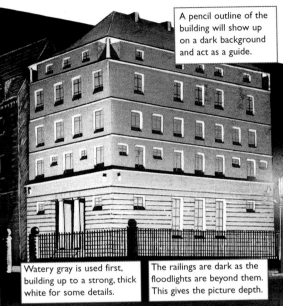

A pencil outline of the building will show up on a dark background and act as a guide.

You could try using lots of tiny dots of color. Denser patches of dots can be used for shadows and details such as windows.

Watery gray is used first, building up to a strong, thick white for some details.

The railings are dark as the floodlights are beyond them. This gives the picture depth.

The shadows

As the building is lit from below, the shadows fall in the opposite direction than normal. Anything jutting out will cast an upward shadow.

Light

Upward shadow

Go to **www.usborne-quicklinks.com** for a link to a Web site where you can see paintings by the most famous impressionist painters.

259

Drawing and using plans

All buildings start as a set of plans. After an architect has designed the building, plans are devised and drawn accurately.

On these pages you can see how to draw your own plans and use them to make a model.

Technical drawing

The neat, detailed drawing style used for plans is called technical drawing.

Building plans are flat drawings of a 3D shape. Some of the tools used for technical drawing are shown below.

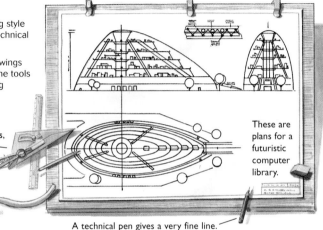

Compasses, set squares and rulers for drawing arcs, angles and straight lines.

A flexi-curve can be adjusted to draw any kind of curve.

These are plans for a futuristic computer library.

A technical pen gives a very fine line.

Drawing plans

There are three main plan-drawing steps.

1. All measurements are calculated and a scale (see below) is set.

2. Information is gathered about all features such as windows, doors, wall thicknesses and even stoves and sinks. Rough plans are then drawn.

3. The finished plan is drawn to scale, using standard symbols for some features. Several elevations (see below) are usually shown.

Scale

A suitable scale is calculated for a plan, depending on the size of the building. A scale of 1:12 means that 1inch on the plan represents 1 foot.

Elevations

Most plans show a building from two or more viewpoints. If the front and the side are shown, for example, these are called the front and side elevations.

260 *Go to www.usborne-quicklinks.com for a link to a Web site where you can see examples of lots of different ways you can draw plans.*

Drawing your home

Follow the steps here to make a plan of the inside of your home.

1. First note the length and width of the rooms and corridors of your home. Use a measuring tape, rather than a ruler.

2. Make a rough sketch to help you position everything. Then set a simple scale to be used on the finished drawing.

Door opens into the room.

3. Measure windows and doors, noting their positions and direction of opening. Note the number of stairs.

4. Do the final drawing. Add features such as the stove.

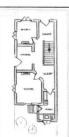

🔲 Stove symbol
🔲 Sink symbol

Making a model

You could invent your own building and make a model of it. You may find it helpful to draw a scale plan and elevations for it first.

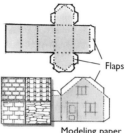

Flaps

Modeling paper

Make sure all shadows go in the same direction.

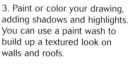

Use a strong glue.

Once you feel confident about drawing plans and making models, you can tackle more complicated shapes.

Make your drawing of the model on thin cardboard so that it stands firmly. You will need scissors and glue.

1. Lay out the building around a base, as shown. Draw flaps down each open side for gluing together later.

2. Now draw details such as doors, windows and roof tiles. You can buy modeling paper of bricks, stones and tiles if you prefer.

3. Paint or color your drawing, adding shadows and highlights. You can use a paint wash to build up a textured look on walls and roofs.

4. Cut the building out. Fold the flaps and glue the building together. Paint a base on a piece of cardboard and glue your building onto that.

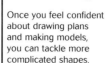

Tips and materials

When learning how to draw, you don't have to spend a lot of money on equipment. Choosing the right drawing materials and paper, and learning some basic techniques will help you make a good start.

Choosing drawing materials

The kind of drawing tool you use depends on the style you want. A pen or pencil, for instance, is best for detailed line drawing. A mixture of some of the items below is ideal.

Pencils range from very hard to very soft (9H to 7B). It is best to buy a hard (2H) and a medium (HB) pencil for lines, and a soft (3B) pencil for shading. H stands for hard and B stands for black.

Felt- or fiber-tip pens can be used for line drawing and coloring. Fiber-tips give a thinner line while felt-tips are good for large areas of color.

Colored pencils can give lines of varying thickness and color strength. They also show up well on colored paper. Some can double as paints.

Wax crayons, pastels, chalks and charcoal can be used for a softer look. They are good for large-scale drawings.

Pens are widely available, ranging from ballpoints to fine technical drawing pens. They are good for all line drawing.

Watercolor paints can be mixed to produce a wide range of colors. Buy two paintbrushes – a medium one for general use and a thin one for detail.

Paper

There is a large range of paper available. Most gift shops sell basic sketch pads, and these are fine for most purposes. The best quality watercolour paper is usually only available from art supply stores. Do not paint on very thin paper.

Loose-leaf plain paper is fine for most drawings.

Rougher sketch paper is better for paint.

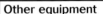

Rough water-color paper is ideal for paint, but expensive.

Other equipment

Rulers with built-in stencils of shapes or lines can be very useful for your drawings.

Cotton swabs can smudge and blend crayons, pastels and chalks.

Plastic erasers remove pencil lines cleanly. Putty erasers can be twisted to reach tiny areas.

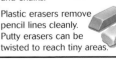

Internet links

For links to more Web sites about buildings and how to draw them, go to the Usborne Quicklinks Web site at **www.usborne-quicklinks.com** and click on the number of the Web site you want to visit.

Web site 1 This photo gallery of buildings is organized by period styles. Click on **Medieval Architecture** to see pictures of medieval castles or on **Cupolas, Domes and Towers** to see some really elaborately decorated buildings.

Web site 2 This huge Web site lists all the greatest buildings from around the world. Click on the name of a famous building or architect for a picture and a description.

Web site 3 You can learn more about different ways to draw perspective at this Web site.

Web site 4 At this Web site you can find out how the Egyptians might have built the pyramids and see photos and detailed plans of these amazing buildings. There are also pictures of items found inside the pyramids.

Web site 5 At this Web site you can see lots of pictures of the Parthenon, the most famous Ancient Greek temple, in Athens.

Web site 6 The Taj Mahal is one of the most distinctive buildings in the world and at this site you can see paintings inspired by India's best-known building.

Web site 7 This is a great site if you are interested in medieval buildings. Click on the picture of the **cathedral** on the map of medieval Reims to see pictures of its intricate stone carving. To see beautiful architectural drawings of a typical French Gothic church, click on **St Rémi**.

Web site 8 Japanese castles look very different from the European ones shown in this book. You can see some wonderful pictures of them at this Web site.

Web site 9 Here you can see a gallery of photos of skyscrapers from around the world. Click on a picture to see it enlarged.

Web site 10 This Web site is a great introduction to architecture including drawings, materials and some unusual building styles and shapes.

Web site 11 This Web site is all about gargoyles, unusual stone carvings seen on many Gothic and modern buildings. There are lots of pictures to inspire you.

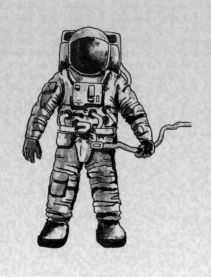

HOW TO DRAW
SPACECRAFT

Emma Fischel and Anita Ganeri

Designed by Mike Pringle, Steve Page, Brian Robertson,
Richard Maddox, Kim Blundell and Chris Gillingwater
Illustrated by Mike Pringle, Gary Mayes, Guy Smith,
Martin Newton, Kim Blundell and Kuo Kang Chen

CONTENTS

266 Drawing spacecraft
268 Rockets
270 Space journey
272 Special techniques
274 The planets
276 Inside a space station
278 On the Moon

280 The future in space
282 Drawing a comic strip
284 Space aliens
285 UFOs
286 Cartoon spacecraft
287 Internet links

Drawing spacecraft

This section shows you how to draw lots of different things associated with space. As well as spacecraft and other space machines, you can see how to draw planet landscapes, aliens, astronauts and even future worlds in space.

Space machines

This section has many ideas for drawing real space machines from rockets and space probes to satellites and space stations. You can see how to use similar ideas to draw imaginary spacecraft. There are also suggestions for drawing aliens and Unidentified Flying Objects (UFOs).

See page 272 for this rocket.

This starship is on page 286.

There are all kinds of UFOs on page 285.

Drawing backgrounds

A dramatic background can help make your picture stand out on the page. There are many suggestions for ways of creating atmospheric backgrounds, such as using comets and meteors on page 271 or planets on pages 274–275.

Fantasy drawing

As space is still largely unexplored, there is plenty of scope for using your imagination to create pictures of life in the future. Pages 280–281 show what life might be like on a planet in the future. On pages 282–283 you can see examples of comic strip art done by science fiction artists, with tips on drawing your own fantasy pictures.

Drawing tips

Drawing in stages

Many of the pictures have step-by-step outlines to help you draw them. Sketch all the outlines in pencil first.

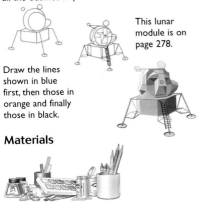

This lunar module is on page 278.

Draw the lines shown in blue first, then those in orange and finally those in black.

Materials

There are many suggestions for coloring materials to use. Pencils, pastels or watercolor paints are good for blended pictures. Pens, poster paints or computer graphic programs are good for bold pictures using solid colors.

Professional techniques

This section gives many examples of techniques used by designers to show how parts of a space machine work or fit together. By following the simple explanations you can see how to give your drawings a really professional look.

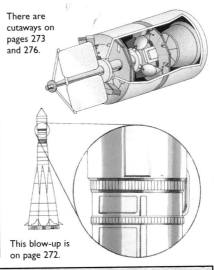

There are cutaways on pages 273 and 276.

This blow-up is on page 272.

Mixing pictures

You could combine realistic and fantasy pictures from this book to create original space scenes. In this picture, for example, realistic astronauts come face to face with an alien on an imaginary planet.

Rockets

On the following four pages there are many different kinds of rockets to draw, from the first rocket to take people to the Moon, to the Space Shuttle. You can also find out about coloring and design techniques used by professional artists.

Drawing a rocket

The rocket on the right can be broken down into simple shapes. Use the steps below to help you get the shapes right. Make the rocket any size you like.

1. Draw the lines shown in pencil first. These are called construction lines. They will help you position the shapes correctly and make them the right size in relation to each other. Next, draw the lines shown in blue.

Construction lines are just a guide, not part of the finished picture.

Start with a line down the middle to get the shapes the same on each side.

2. Draw in the lines shown in orange. Then add the details shown in black. Go over the finished outline in fine black pen, then erase the construction lines.

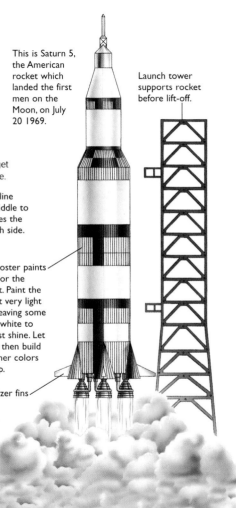

This is Saturn 5, the American rocket which landed the first men on the Moon, on July 20 1969.

Launch tower supports rocket before lift-off.

Use poster paints to color the rocket. Paint the rocket very light gray, leaving some areas white to suggest shine. Let it dry, then build up other colors on top.

Stabilizer fins

268

Using a grid

If you want to copy a spacecraft picture from a magazine, book or photograph but would like to make it a different size from the original, try this grid method.

1. Draw a grid of equal-sized squares on tracing paper. Make the grid big enough to cover the picture you want to copy.

2. Put the grid over the picture. Draw another grid on a sheet of paper. Make the squares bigger than those on the tracing paper grid to enlarge the picture, or smaller to reduce it.

3. Look at each square on the tracing paper grid and copy the shape in it onto the same square on your second grid. Finally, erase the grid lines.

The Space Shuttle

The first Space Shuttle was launched by the USA in 1981. A Shuttle takes off like a rocket but lands horizontally like a plane. Its fuel tanks are jettisoned (released) once the fuel is used up. To draw the picture below, first copy the shape in the box.

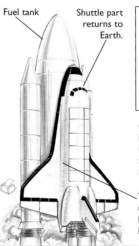

Fuel tank

Shuttle part returns to Earth.

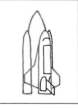

Color the Shuttle in colored pencils, using darker shading to show its rounded shape.

This way of shading using short, slanting lines is called hatching.

Cartoon rockets

To draw these cartoon rockets, copy the shapes in pencil then go over the outlines in black felt-tip pen. Use bright colors to fill in the shapes. Rockets need to travel very fast to go into space. To do this, they must reach speeds of at least 25,000mph.

If a rocket does not go fast enough, it falls back to Earth.

Space journey

Here you can see how to draw the various stages of a rocket's journey through space. There are also tips on creating a dramatic background.

Rocket zooming into space

Objects look smaller the further away they are. This is called perspective.

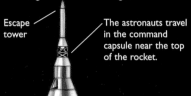

Escape tower

The astronauts travel in the command capsule near the top of the rocket.

Third stage

Second stage

First stage jettisoned

A Rocket built in one piece would be too heavy to gain enough speed to enter space.

Meteors are pieces of rock. At about 80km (50 miles) from Earth they burn up, making streaks of light which are called shooting stars.

First stage

A multi-stage rocket

Rockets are used to launch satellites and manned spacecraft into space. As rockets need to reach huge speeds in order to enter space (see page 269), they are built in sections, called stages. Each stage is jettisoned when its fuel is used up, making the rest of the rocket lighter and faster. The engines of the next stage fire, giving the rocket more power and speed.

The vanishing point is the furthest point the eye can see.

Capsule returning to earth

To draw these spacecraft in perspective, first draw three lines meeting at a point.

This is called the vanishing point. Draw in the shapes between the lines.

Distances in space are measured in light years. A light year is the distance traveled by light in one year, about 6 trillion miles.

Apollo spacecraft

Third stage separates

Second stage jettisoned

Comets are balls of ice and dust. Comets travelling near the Sun have long tails of gases and dust released from them by the Sun's heat.

Drawing the background

Here are some suggestions for ways to color in a space background, using a mixture of watercolors and chalks on a sheet of dark blue or black paper.

To draw star clusters, dip a brush into white paint. Flick the paint on to the paper with your finger. Add crosses and smudges of chalk.

Draw the comets in white paint. Use a thick blob of paint for the body. Then add quite thick, dry streaks for the tail.

To draw meteors, start by painting the shapes white. Let this dry, then add layers of light and dark brown paint on top.

Special techniques

Blow-ups

The picture below shows a blow-up. Professional designers use this technique to pull out one part of a machine and show it in a lot of detail. To draw this blow-up, follow the steps below.

1. First draw the outline of the whole rocket in pencil. Draw a small circle around the part to be blown up.

2. Draw two straight lines extending from the circle, then draw a larger circle between them.

This blow-up shows details of the Russian Vostok spacecraft.

You could use a different shape to frame the blow-up, such as a square or rectangle.

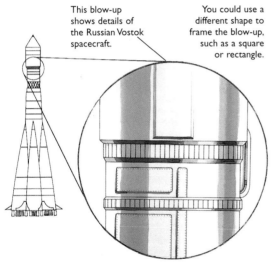

3. Next, fill in the details of the part that is blown up inside the circle frame with pencil.

4. Go over the lines in black pen. Then paint the blow-up with blue and gray watercolor.

Exploded drawings

Exploded drawings are used to show how parts of a machine fit together. Parts are drawn slightly away from their true position to show how they are joined to each other.

This is a picture of Apollo 11.

Arrows show exactly where the parts fit together.

Use long strokes of colored pencil for the outer shell.

Try figuring out your own exploded drawings using the ideas above. You could use some of the machines shown later in this section, such as the satellite on the facing page or the lunar module on page 278.

Drawing a cutaway

This picture is called a cutaway. Cutaways leave out part of a machine's outer shell to show what is inside it. They are often used by spacecraft designers to show how the equipment on board is to be carried. See how to draw a cutaway space station on pages 276–277.

To draw this cutaway, pencil in the outline of the satellite's shell and draw a line around the area which will form the cutaway section. Add more details to both sections, then go over the pencil lines in black. Color the satellite with felt-tip pens.

Comstar I is a communications satellite.

Radio equipment beams signals from one place to another.

To show the contrast between the two parts, you could color in one section only and just outline the other.

The white line shows the cutaway section.

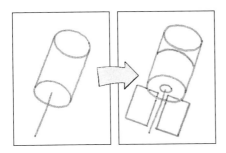

Satellites

A satellite is any object in space which orbits a larger object. It can be natural, like Earth which orbits the Sun, or artificial, like the ones on this page.

Comstar 1

To draw this picture, first copy the outline shapes in pencil. Color the body with felt-tip pens and add the final details with fine, black lines.

Use thick felt-tip pens for the planet.

A white area suggests a metallic shine on the satellite.

Go to **www.usborne-quicklinks.com** for a link to a Web site with a diagram of a satellite to help you get the details right. Click on any of the labels for an explanation.

The planets

Earth is in a part of space called the Solar System. This is made up of the Sun, nine planets which orbit it, their moons and a band of rocks called the asteroid belt. Below, you can find out more about planets and ways of drawing them.

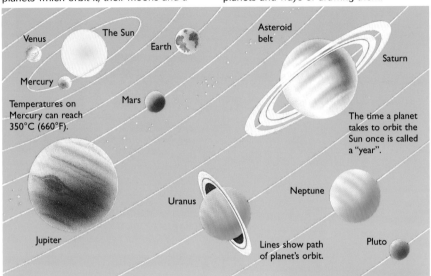

Venus

The Sun

Earth

Asteroid belt

Saturn

Mercury

Temperatures on Mercury can reach 350°C (660°F).

Mars

The time a planet takes to orbit the Sun once is called a "year".

Jupiter

Uranus

Neptune

Pluto

Lines show path of planet's orbit.

Computer graphics

You can use a drawing program on a computer to draw bright pictures using solid blocks of color and simple shapes. The picture on the right was drawn using a popular program called Microsoft® Paint.

The advantage of drawing on a computer is that you can change the colors or size of your picture and even move parts of it around without having to start again. When you are pleased with your picture, you can print it out.

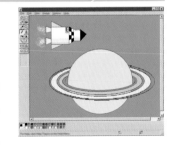

Drawing the planets

If you don't have a computer you can achieve dramatic effects using shades of colored pencils.

Jupiter

The red patch is a huge hurricane, about three times as big as Earth.

Use pale red and orange with darker bands on top. Add shadows around the bottom half of the planet.

Saturn

Saturn's rings are made up of millions of ice and rock particles.

Gases on Saturn's surface make bands of different colors. Show this with contrasting shades.

Uranus

Uranus takes 84 Earth years to orbit the Sun.

Uranus looks green because of clouds of methane gas swirling around it. Shade this planet with green and yellow.

Planetary probes

Planetary probes are unmanned spacecraft, launched into space by rockets. Cameras on board send back pictures of a planet's surface.

Mariner

Here you can see how to draw the Mariner probe, which took photographs of the surface of Mars.

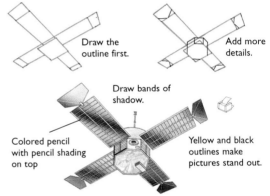

Draw the outline first.

Add more details.

Draw bands of shadow.

Colored pencil with pencil shading on top

Yellow and black outlines make pictures stand out.

Surface of Mars

Use yellow to show clouds.

Mars is called the Red Planet because its surface is made up of red rocks. Recently, Viking probes have landed on Mars to test its atmosphere and soil. They carry remote-controlled cars, called rovers, which explore the surface of the planet.

Go to **www.usborne-quicklinks.com** for a link to a Web site where you can see pictures of the surface of Mars taken by a surface rover.

Inside a space station

A space station is a type of satellite launched by a rocket. It carries a crew and equipment for doing scientific research impossible to do on Earth. It also studies how people are affected by spending a long time in space.

Skylab

Skylab was launched in 1973. Among other equipment, it carried a telescope to study the Sun. Here you can see how to draw this cutaway of Skylab by breaking it down into simple shapes. Start by copying the blue outline.

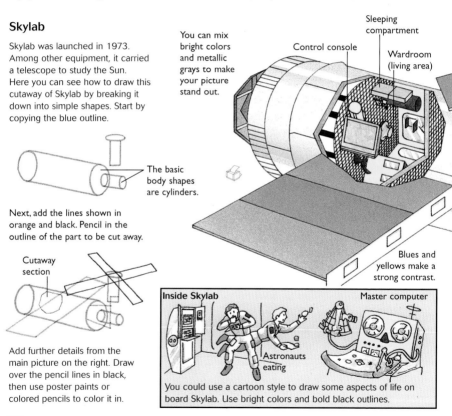

You can mix bright colors and metallic grays to make your picture stand out.

The basic body shapes are cylinders.

Next, add the lines shown in orange and black. Pencil in the outline of the part to be cut away.

Cutaway section

Add further details from the main picture on the right. Draw over the pencil lines in black, then use poster paints or colored pencils to color it in.

Sleeping compartment

Control console

Wardroom (living area)

Blues and yellows make a strong contrast.

Inside Skylab

Master computer

Astronauts eating

You could use a cartoon style to draw some aspects of life on board Skylab. Use bright colors and bold black outlines.

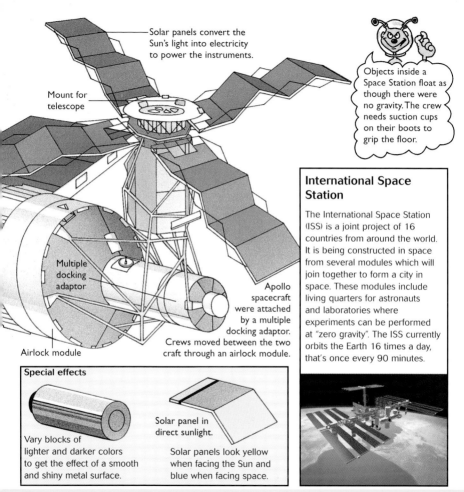

Solar panels convert the Sun's light into electricity to power the instruments.

Mount for telescope

Objects inside a Space Station float as though there were no gravity. The crew needs suction cups on their boots to grip the floor.

International Space Station

The International Space Station (ISS) is a joint project of 16 countries from around the world. It is being constructed in space from several modules which will join together to form a city in space. These modules include living quarters for astronauts and laboratories where experiments can be performed at "zero gravity". The ISS currently orbits the Earth 16 times a day, that's once every 90 minutes.

Multiple docking adaptor

Apollo spacecraft were attached by a multiple docking adaptor. Crews moved between the two craft through an airlock module.

Airlock module

Special effects

Vary blocks of lighter and darker colors to get the effect of a smooth and shiny metal surface.

Solar panel in direct sunlight.

Solar panels look yellow when facing the Sun and blue when facing space.

Go to www.usborne-quicklinks.com for a link to a Web site all about the ISS and how the modules will fit together.

On the Moon

The Moon is over 236,000 miles away, but it is Earth's closest neighbor in space. Since unmanned lunar probes were launched in the 1950s, people have landed on the Moon and we now know more about it. Here you can see how to draw the Moon's surface and machines which have landed on it.

Lunar Module

To enlarge this shape you could use a grid (see page 269).

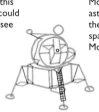

The Lunar Module took astronauts from the USA Apollo spacecraft to the Moon's surface.

To draw the Lunar Module, follow the outlines above. Draw the lines shown in blue first.

Next draw the lines shown in orange, then add the further details shown in black to your picture.

Fill in the shapes with bright blocks of color. To make the picture stand out further, you could outline it in black.

The Lunar Rover was transported to the Moon by Apollo 15 in 1971.

The first man on the Moon was Neil Armstrong. He landed on July 20 1969.

The surface of the Moon is very dry and dusty. To get a grainy look, put a sheet of sandpaper under your picture when you color it.

Moon craters

The surface of the Moon is pitted with millions of craters. These were probably caused by meteorites crashing onto the surface.

278 Go to www.usborne-quicklinks.com for a link to a Web site where you can see pictures of Apollo 11 landing on the Moon.

Seen from the Moon, the Earth does not always look perfectly round. This is because part of it is often hidden in shadow.

The Module was covered in a substance like foil to protect it from the Sun's intense heat, so color it silver.

Astronauts bounce along the ground because gravity on the Moon is six times less than on Earth, so they seem six times lighter.

There is no wind or rain on the Moon, so astronauts' footprints will never be worn away.

Use colored pencils to draw the craters. To show the insides, use dark pencil shading and white highlights.

Spacesuits

As the Moon has no air, astronauts have to wear special suits with tanks providing them with oxygen to breathe. The suits also protect them from the cold on the Moon.

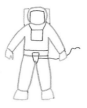

Use the outline above to help you draw this astronaut.

Color the spacesuit in watercolor paint. Use highlights to show the shine on the material.

The future in space

This picture shows what life might be like on an imaginary planet in the future. Although this is a fantasy picture, many of the things in it are based on scientific theory about advances that may be possible by then.

The picture is painted in poster paints. Use pale colors for things in the background and darker colors for closer objects. Dabs of yellow look like tiny windows and white paint is used for highlights and reflections.

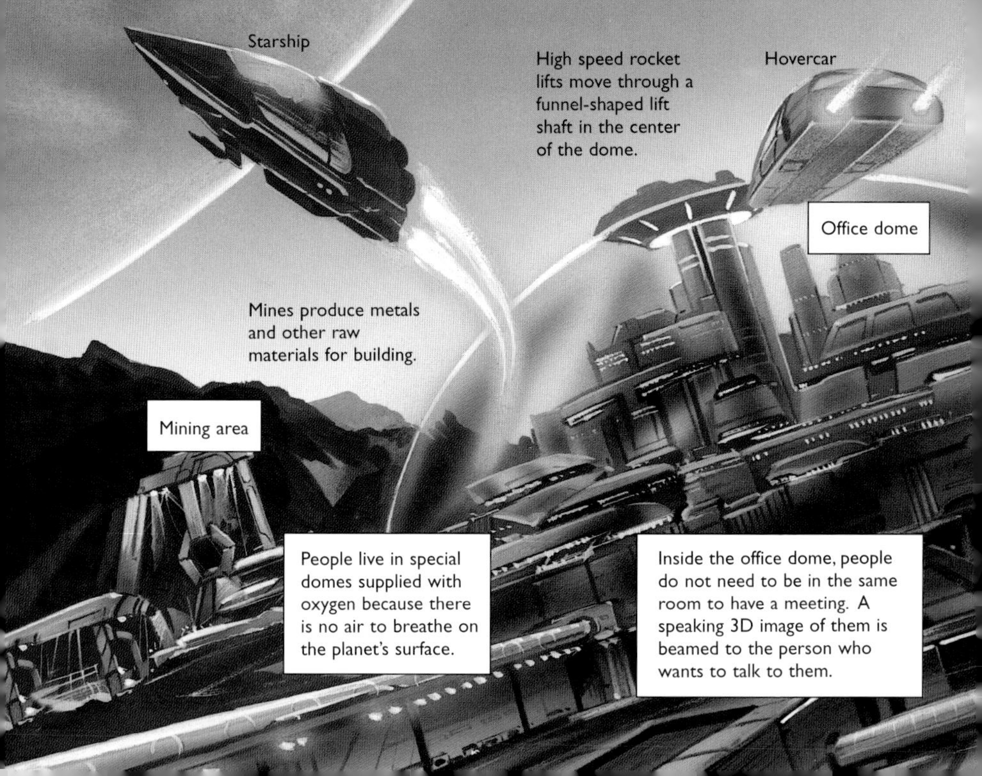

Starship

High speed rocket lifts move through a funnel-shaped lift shaft in the center of the dome.

Hovercar

Office dome

Mines produce metals and other raw materials for building.

Mining area

People live in special domes supplied with oxygen because there is no air to breathe on the planet's surface.

Inside the office dome, people do not need to be in the same room to have a meeting. A speaking 3D image of them is beamed to the person who wants to talk to them.

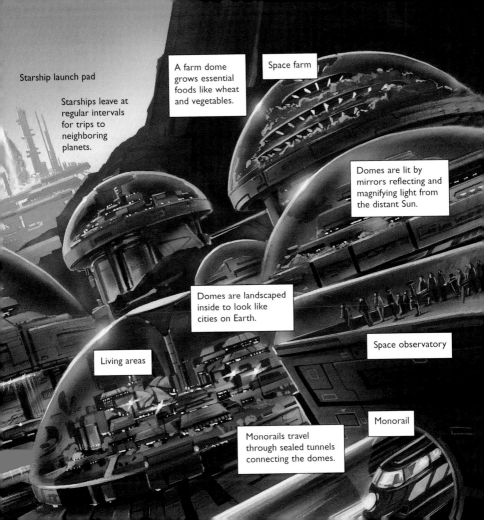

Starship launch pad

Starships leave at regular intervals for trips to neighboring planets.

A farm dome grows essential foods like wheat and vegetables.

Space farm

Domes are lit by mirrors reflecting and magnifying light from the distant Sun.

Domes are landscaped inside to look like cities on Earth.

Space observatory

Living areas

Monorail

Monorails travel through sealed tunnels connecting the domes.

Drawing a comic strip

Here you can see how to build up your own science fiction comic strip, starting from a basic story idea. There are also tips for making your strip look really professional.

The plot

Start by thinking up a plot. Try to keep it short. Make sure the story starts off with lots of action and ends with a strong punchline.

In a comic strip, the pictures are just as important as the text. They should be action-packed and exciting to look at.

PLOT
1. VILLAIN AND ROBOT ARMY ATTACK PLANET.
2. PLANET LEADER AND PEOPLE MEET.
3. HERO ARRIVES WITH SECRET WEAPON.
4. HERO MEETS VILLAIN.
5. SECRET WEAPON REVEALED AS SHRINKING GUN.
6. VILLAIN SHRUNK AND DEFEATED

This is the plot for the comic strip on the right-hand page.

Creating characters

You need to give your characters strong personalities and draw them with slightly exaggerated features so they are easy to recognize in each frame. Here are the main characters in the comic strip on the right.

The hero

This is Captain Kovac, the hero of the story.

The villain

This is his arch-enemy, the evil Suberon.

Frames

The events in a comic strip are split into episodes and a picture is drawn for each one. These are called frames.

You can draw box rules freehand or use a ruler.

First, sketch out your ideas for each frame and draw in the boxes. You may need to try out several ideas. Add details to your sketches.

Speech bubbles

Use bubbles for spoken words, thoughts, and even sound effects. Do the lettering in capital letters to make it easy to read.

THERE IS NO HOPE!
... SUDDENLY

The shape of the letters can also suggest sounds.

The bubbles can be different shapes and sizes.

SOON ALL THIS WILL BE MINE!

EEEK!

Thought bubbles are shown with rings, not arrows.

People read from left to right and top to bottom.

The finished strip

Here you can see how all the elements on the previous page are combined to make a comic strip.

Space aliens

Space exploration has not been able to prove that life exists on other planets – yet. As no one knows what alien life forms would look like, you can make them as unusual as you like. An alien could look similar to a human being, but on a planet where conditions are different from Earth, its limbs and senses may have developed in strange ways. Here you can see some suggestions for drawing humanoid aliens.

Metal Martian

No visible ears

Four hands, but only three fingers on each

To draw this alien, first use a pencil to copy the blue outline above on the left, then add the lines shown in orange. Fill in the shapes of the arms and legs and erase the pencil lines inside them. Copy the alien's clothes from the main picture and draw in its features. Go over the outline in black.

In 1955, someone claimed to see a goblin-like alien peering through a kitchen window in Kentucky USA. It was only 3 feet high, with pointed ears and big, bulging eyes.

Aliens under pressure

Aliens on a low gravity planet would be tall and thin. High gravity would force them into shorter, squatter shapes.

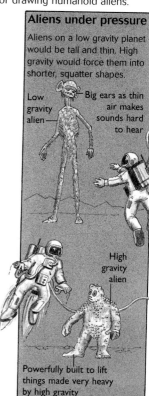

Low gravity alien

Big ears as thin air makes sounds hard to hear

High gravity alien

Powerfully built to lift things made very heavy by high gravity

UFOs

Many people claim to have seen alien spacecraft in the sky and even landing on Earth. These spacecraft are called Unidentified Flying Objects, or UFOs. Some can be explained scientifically; others cannot. UFOs come in many shapes.

Flying saucers

The most common type of UFO is called a flying saucer. Not all flying saucers are saucer-shaped though. They can also be torpedo-shaped or look like balls or spheres of light.

Use the outline shape below to help you draw a flying saucer.

Add more details, such as windows around the side and lights underneath the body. Color the saucer in watercolor, as shown here, or in colored pencil.

Draw the saucer bathed in a strange, yellow light.

Actual sighting?

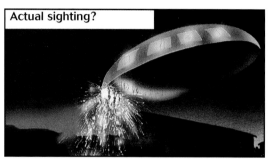

The UFO above was reported in Marseilles, France in October 1952. A pale blue light shone from its windows and sparks showered from one end. Use the outline to help you draw it.

Silhouettes and shadows

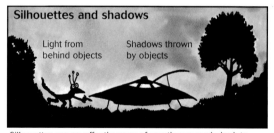

Light from behind objects

Shadows thrown by objects

Silhouettes are an effective way of creating an eerie look to your UFO pictures. Imagine a strong light from behind trees, spacecraft or even alien figures. Draw the outlines of the shadows in pencil, then fill in the shapes with black paint or ink. Make the background very pale to give a good contrast.

Go to **www.usborne-quicklinks.com** for a link to a Web site where you can find more ideas for art projects with aliens or spacecraft.

Cartoon spacecraft

Here are some suggestions for cartoon spacecraft to add to your space scenes. You can add your own ideas to the spacecraft such as logos* or alien passengers.

Using some of the basic shapes for the real spacecraft shown in this section, you can make up machines like the ones below.

Color them any way you like and add extra details like lights, engines, wing and tail fins and smoke trails.

Logos

Here are some ideas for logos to add to your spacecraft. You could design your own logos based on the name of your spacecraft or your initials.

Internet links

For links to more Web sites about spacecraft and aliens and how to draw them, go to the Usborne Quicklinks Web site at **www.usborne-quicklinks.com** and click on the number of the Web site you want to visit.

Web site 1 Go to this Web site for fun space-related information, images and games.

Web site 2 This site is packed with pictures and information about spacecraft, including a Space Shuttle animation and images of satellites, space probes and more.

Web site 3 The Hubble Web site is packed with fun facts and games. Click on **Galaxies Galore** to see images of distant galaxies taken by the Hubble Telescope. Play "Build our Milky Way" to see what makes up our own galaxy, the Milky Way. For even more games, click on **Galaxy Games**.

Web site 4 This gallery contains hundreds of photographs of rockets, shuttles, satellites and probes. You can enlarge any image by clicking on it.

Web site 5 Click on the names of different parts of the Space Shuttle to see how they fit together and to read more about them.

Web site 6 At this site, you can download instructions that show you how to build your own space station out of drink bottles.

Web site 7 At this Web site you'll find instructions on how to draw different aliens and how to create 3D aliens out of a variety of materials.

Web site 8 Here you can see pictures of craters on the Moon and on the Earth. You can also find out how craters are formed.

Web site 9 Artists have been fascinated by space travel for a long time. At this Web site you can see pictures of imaginary spacecraft dating from as early as 1865.

Web site 10 These online space comics will give you lots of ideas for creating one of your own.

Web site 11 You'll find lots of pictures and information about meteorites, galaxies and asteroids at this Web site about astronomy.

Web site 12 At this Web site, you can find out how space suits work and see a photograph of a future space suit.

Index

aliens, 50, 56-57, 267, 284
animals, 34, 121-143
  big, 134-135
  cuddly, 139
  farm, 130-131
  prehistoric, 28-29
  shapes, 123, 231
  wild, 136-137
astronauts, 91, 267, 276, 279

bicycles, 86-87
bird's-eye view, 8, 9, 37
blocking, 177
blueprints, 92
borders, 17, 19, 218, 223, 237
buildings, 241-263
  ancient, 252-253
  period styles, 245

caricatures, 2, 12, 147, 164
cars, 76-79
cartoons, 1-23
  aliens, 267, 284
  alien's house, 248
  animals, 22, 122, 125, 127,
  129, 130, 131, 133, 134, 135,
  136, 137, 138, 140, 141, 142
  ballerina, 12
  bicycles, 87
  boxer, 12
  buildings, 243, 248, 258
  burglar, 12, 13
  cars, 79
  castle, 248
  cats, 188-189
  cave people, 42, 43, 44, 45
  chef, 12

cartoons (cont.)
  dinosaurs, 27, 31, 33, 36, 37,
  38-39, 42-43, 44, 45
  expressions, 2, 3, 6, 7, 17, 103
  faces, 3, 6, 7, 165
  ghosts, 98, 103, 114-115
  horses, 129, 210-211
  lettering, 11, 16, 42, 44, 282
  machines, 74
  people, 3-13
  planes, 85
  rockets, 269
  sound effects, 17, 19, 20-21,
  44, 282
  spacecraft, 286
  space station, 276
  special effects, 18, 20-21,
  speech bubbles, 16, 17, 19,
  20, 42, 282
  stick figures, 4, 5, 10, 12
  trains, 83
  vampires, 116
cartouches, 223, 227
castles, 246-247
cats, 126-127, 169-191
  basic shapes, 170, 171, 178
  179, 181, 183, 187, 188
  big cats, 132-133, 171, 186-187
  fur and markings, 124-125,
  176-177
  kittens, 184-185, 189, 190
chalks, 56, 75, 82, 87, 94, 102,
  111, 125, 271
charcoal, 57, 75, 82, 94
charts, 219
cobwebs, 109, 112
collage, 163

colored pencils, 3, 53, 68,
  70, 75, 81, 87, 90, 92, 103,
  106, 107, 109, 117, 118, 123,
  124, 125, 126, 128, 137, 138,
  141, 147, 148, 161, 177, 197,
  200, 203, 204, 206, 213,
  224, 258-259, 269, 275, 276
colors, 4, 5, 17, 28, 156, 160
  artist's, 28, 34, 35
  cold and warm, 156, 162
comic strips, 2, 14, 16-17,
  18-19, 21, 42-43, 159,
  266, 282-283
comic style, 243
composition, 190, 256
computer drawing, 165, 274
cross-hatching, 75, 177, 256

dinosaurs, 25-47, 50, 52-53
  flying, 36-37, 53
  imaginary, 31
  moving, 37, 45
  simple shapes, 28
  skeletons, 26, 38
  skin textures, 29, 32, 34, 38,
  46, 53
dragons, 50, 60, 62-63, 237
dwarfs, 66

elevations, 260

fantasy,
  buildings, 248-249
  castle game, 238
  machines, 74, 92-93
  map, 236-237
fixative sprays, 68, 94, 99

floor plans, 238

foreshortening, 9, 65, 153, 157, 179, 183, 207

frames, 16, 17, 18, 19, 41, 42, 43, 282

gargoyles, 51

ghosts, 54-55, 97-119, 251
  Chinese, 106
  cut-out, 101
  Egyptian khu, 107
  genie, 105
  headless, 104
  hound, 107
  human, 102-105
  Japanese, 106
  kelpie, 107
  pirate, 102
  poltergeists, 113
  seeing, 103, 115
  see-through, 104, 105
  shadowy, 100
  shapes, 100
  sheet, 103, 114
  train, 108-109

giants, 64

globe, 230

goblins, 67

grid, using a, 27, 74, 232, 269

hatching, 21, 69, 75, 177, 269

haunted houses, 98, 110-113, 250-251

horses, 128-129, 193-215
  basic shapes, 196, 202, 205, 206, 210
  breeds, 212-213
  details, 208
  foals, 199, 213

horses (cont.)
  heads, 198-199
  in action, 200-209

impressionism, 243, 258

Internet links 23, 47, 71, 95, 119, 143, 167, 191, 215, 239, 263, 287

machines, 73-95
  inventions, 92-93

maps, 217-239
  contours, 225
  enlarging, 232
  fantasy, 236-237
  old, 226-227
  route, 223, 234
  symbols, 218, 222, 224-225, 232, 233
  world, 226, 230-231

masking fluid, 38, 39

materials, 15, 50, 68-69, 74, 75, 147, 177, 194, 262, 267

models,
  building, 261
  dinosaur, 32

monsters, 31, 49-71
  famous, 50
  man-made, 60-61
  sea, 34-35, 58-59
  shapes, 50, 52

motorcycles, 87

octopus, 58

ogre, 65

paint, 52, 57, 58, 59, 62, 69, 70, 74, 75, 90, 91
  gouache, 110, 147, 194, 208

paint (cont.)
  poster, 104, 108, 110, 118, 147, 268, 276, 280
  watercolor, 28, 32, 38, 39, 46, 91, 100, 101, 104, 105, 107, 109, 110, 122, 123, 124, 126, 130, 131, 133, 134, 137, 139, 141, 147, 160, 177, 194, 202, 219, 262, 271, 272

paintbrushes, 15

paper, 74, 219, 262
  Bristol, 15

Pegasus, 214

pencils, 3, 5, 9, 13, 15, 57, 68, 69, 99, 100, 124, 147, 194, 219, 262

pens, 15, 19, 147, 154-155, 242
  ballpoint, 106, 108, 109, 118
  felt-tip, 3, 4, 15, 36, 52, 54, 69, 74, 75, 87, 101, 103, 105, 106, 107, 108, 109, 116, 117, 122, 125, 127, 129, 134, 147, 154, 155, 162, 163, 164, 194, 210, 258, 269, 273

people, 145-167
  bodies, 150-151, 152, 160, 162, 163
  faces, 148-149, 154-155, 161
  portraits, 148, 154-155
  profiles, 3, 41, 149

perspective, 11, 13, 65, 67, 76, 83, 247, 250, 255, 257, 271

planes, 84-85, 257

planets, 274-275

plans, 260-261

printing, 105

robots, 88-89

rockets, 266, 268-269, 270, 272

satellites, 228, 229, 273
scale, 218, 220, 221, 225, 237, 260
science fiction art, 266, 280-283
ship, 81
silhouettes, 11, 20, 21, 84, 255, 285
skeleton, 66
sketches, 122, 146, 150, 152, 160, 171, 220, 244-245, 256
  colouring, 160, 245
skylines, 245, 255
skyscrapers, 254-255
space, 90
  backgrounds, 266, 271

space (cont.)
  machines, 90-91
  scenes, 56, 57, 267
  suits, 279
spacecraft, 265-287
  Apollo, 91, 271, 272, 277, 278
  lunar module, 91, 278
  Space Shuttle, 90, 269
  space stations, 91, 276-277
stencils, 46
stippling, 69, 177
super-hero's view, 254

technical drawing, 260
tractor, 80
trains, 82-83, 257
troll, 65

UFOs, 266, 285

vampires, 14, 98, 114, 116-118
  Dracula, 98, 118

washes, 28, 29, 33, 34, 35, 36, 38, 46, 59, 69, 104, 105, 133, 242-243, 259
wax crayons, 53, 56, 57, 63, 69, 90, 101, 104
werewolf, 70, 117
witches, 67
worm's-eye view, 9, 33, 247, 255

yacht, 81
yeti, 70

ACKNOWLEDGEMENTS

Edited by Ruth Brocklehurst, Emma Helbrough, Mairi MacKinnon and Anna Milbourne. Cover design by Russell Punter. With thanks to Katarina Dragoslavic, Natacha Goransky and Sarah Sherley-Price.
Ancient Babylonian map (page 226) courtesy of The British Museum. Map of the world according to Ptolemy (page 226) © Gianni Dagli Orti/CORBIS. Antique map of New York (page 227) courtesy of The British Library. Aerial photograph of Wolverhampton (page 228) courtesy of Wolverhampton City Council. Satellite image of Sacramento (page 228) courtesy of Digital Vision. Satellite image of Hurricane Andrew (page 229) courtesy of NASA. Space image of Mars (page 229) courtesy of NASA/JPL/Malin Space Science Systems. Space photograph of star nebula (page 229) courtesy of Digital Vision. ISS Photo (page 277) courtesy of Digital Vision. Microsoft® Paint and Microsoft® Windows® are either registered trademarks or trademarks of Microsoft Corporation in the United States and/or other countries.
Screen shots used with permission from Microsoft Corporation.